Amsterdam

Amsterdam

Text by Lindsay Bennett
Photography: Pete Bennett except page 31 by Jon Davison
Cover photograph by Frans Lemmens/Gettyimages
Layout: Media Content Marketing, Inc.
Cartography by Ortelius Design
Managing Editor: Tony Halliday

CONTACTING THE EDITORS
Every effort has been made to provide accurate information in this publication, but changes are inevitable. The publisher cannot be responsible for any resulting loss, inconvenience or injury. We would appreciate it if readers would call our attention to any errors or outdated information by contacting Berlitz Publishing, PO Box 7910, London SE1 1WE, England. Fax: (44) 20 7403 0290;
e-mail: berlitz@apaguide.demon.co.uk

010/302 RP

CONTENTS

- A (☛) in the text denotes a highly recommended sight

Amsterdam

AMSTERDAM AND ITS PEOPLE

There's no other city on earth like Amsterdam. It is a city of superlatives, having more canals than Venice and more bridges than Paris. It is also one of the prettiest in Europe. The more than 50 museums—featuring everything from the worlds most prominent artists, to the history of hemp—quench the thirst for even the most ardent culture buff, and with 6,000 buildings from the 16th, 17th, and 18th centuries, the reflections of its illustrious history happily ripple on into the 21st century. However, the lure of Amsterdam's bricks and mortar is only part of its excitement. Its contemporary culture is vibrant—it's definitely not a city stuck in the past, and the people are open-minded, easygoing, and opinionated but also down to earth and welcoming to visitors.

Amsterdam is situated in the north of The Netherlands and was set where the outlet of the Amstel River meets the salty tidal waters of the Zuider Zee. With little dry land to build on, exactly why a small group of settlers chose this unpromising spot is difficult to understand. Yet it proved to be an excellent decision because Amsterdammers (as the natives of Amsterdam are called) soon came to control the waters of the river, and the trade which flowed along it. By the 17th century, Amsterdam had become arguably the richest city in the world, at the center of a huge Dutch colonial empire. It traded in spices, rum, and sugar cane among other commodities, and its residents demanded only the best. The Amsterdam of this period —called the Golden Age—forms the heart of today's city.

Without doubt, the initial lure of the city is its numerous historic buildings. The lines of tall, narrow houses with their pretty gables rest beside picture-perfect tree-lined canals. They are connected by ornate iron bridges and cobbled walkways, which have changed little for over 300 years, in fact, since they felt the footfall of such inhabitants as the artist Rembrandt and explorer Abel Tasman, who gave his name to Tasmania.

Amsterdam is a wonderful city for visitors. Small enough to stroll around, and with the canal side streets too narrow for tour buses, you can't drive past all the best attractions at high speed. Here, there is no glass window between you and reality. You have to feel the summer sun, or see your breath on a crisp winter morning as you step out to see what Amsterdam is all about. If you take a canal tour, the quiet boats allow you to float slowly along, away from the noise of the modern world.

The museums could keep you busy for weeks. Art collections, historic houses, and memorials to heroes and heroines can all be found here. For entertainment after the sun sets, there are over 40 different performances in the city every evening. The Netherlands National Opera and National Ballet are based here, and there are numerous orchestral, musical, and comedy venues, along with revues and dance shows. Amsterdam also plays host to one of the most dynamic club scenes in Europe, with several major venues drawing thousands of young people to the city.

Yet if the façades of the buildings hark back to the past, the interiors do not. Internet banking, interactive information points, and resource recycling advice centers—the concepts of today are alive and thriving all around the city. This is no historic ghost town, the city brims with people. Its houses are still lived in (although most are now apartments rather than single-family homes), and its streets filled with bakeries, delicatessens, and wine merchants where people drop in to buy dinner on the way home in the evenings. It's all part of the fascinating dichotomy you find at every turn here. The city strides into the future while still holding hands with the past.

The historic heart of Amsterdam has remained unchanged mainly because of people power. As in most cities in the world, during the second part of the 20th century property developers eyed the old canal houses with relish. The price of land was soaring, and developers could make a tidy profit by demolishing them and replacing them with something modern. Unfashionable buildings, such as the warehouses of the old docks, were simply left to the elements, deemed to be worthless. Amsterdammers, though, had other ideas. They went out onto the streets to fight for their city, barricading historic houses and occupying empty buildings in the warehouse district.

This was typical of the populace, and it wasn't the first time; in fact Amsterdammers have been standing up for what they believe in for centuries. When Protestants were persecuted in the 16th century, they flocked here from all around Europe to take

When in Amsterdam, hop on a bicycle! Amsterdammers favor this mode of transport above all others.

City of canals—a typical Amsterdam scene of gabled homes overlooking the water.

refuge. During WWII, the dock workers of Amsterdam went on strike as an act of protest against the treatment of the Jews in the city. Although in the end the protest was futile, it shows the strength of feeling and social awareness that pervades every part of society here. Now, at the beginning of the 21st century, Amsterdam now has over 100 different nationalities living within the city boundaries, a situation which could be fraught with difficulty and strain. Yet here it only adds to the cultural richness built up over centuries of exploration and trade.

Amsterdammers seem to have the ability to find creative solutions to the problems of their world. When there wasn't enough housing on the land, they looked at the empty canals and decided that houseboats would help. There are now over 2,500 on the waterways of the city. When cars became a problem in the old town they gave the bicycle priority, and now there are over 1,000,000 on the streets—and an estimated 30,000 at the bottom of the canal system at any one time! You'll quickly learn to listen for the warning bells and stand clear as their riders pedal by.

Perhaps the most widely publicized acts of tolerance in recent history have been in the areas of sex and drugs.

Amsterdammers looked at feasible and practical responses to the issues, and decriminalized some aspects of both. This does not make the city one huge den of iniquity and these areas *are* still controlled and regulated; in fact, you could visit Amsterdam and be quite unaware of these activities. There's just a recognition here that provided no harm comes to you or others around you, then you should be free, as an adult, to make your own choices.

Amsterdammers fight for everyone's rights against oppression, or the right of David to stand against the faceless Goliath of bureaucracy. In fact in Amsterdam several thousand Davids get together to form a pressure group, and Goliath has to sit up and take notice. This doesn't mean that Amsterdam is utopia—it is a city of 21st-century pressures, particularly with continuing problems of traffic and litter—but it does mean that the problems are faced realistically, debated passionately by the whole community, and agreed solutions are put into action. When the solutions don't work (as they often don't) the whole process starts over again. It is all seen as part of a huge learning curve.

Of course, Amsterdammers don't spend all their time waving protest banners. They are as industrious and hardworking as their forefathers. They enjoy galleries and exhibitions as much as the visitors do—in fact it can be very hard to get tickets for performances because of local demand. On weekends they head to the parks to picnic, or out of the city in large groups to do more cycling. They eat out in restaurants and cafés—where they have over 50 different types of cuisine to choose from. They love to socialize, and bars—particularly the famous "brown bars"—are the place where they meet, usually to put the world to rights. In summer they sit out with a drink as bar owners put out tables in the squares and on street corners. Sit at a table and you'll soon find your-

Street action—If you need to refuel, look no further than the ubiquitous patat frites (thick-cut fries) snack shack.

self engaged in conversation (most Amsterdammers speak good English). Within an hour you'll feel like a local.

Amsterdam has many facets, almost as many as the diamonds for which the city is famous. Yet these seem to amalgamate into a coherent whole. It is a city of history, which shouts from every gable and street corner; a city of culture —of museums, and musicians, and artists; a city of learning with a large university; a city of trade with banking at its core; a multi-ethnic city of over 100 different nationalities; a city of "live and let live" as minority groups are able to flourish and innovative ideas to develop; and of course, a city of tourism, with over 32 million visitors per year. The beauty of its buildings is undisputed, but it is the sum of all these parts that makes Amsterdam an unforgettable city to visit.

A BRIEF HISTORY

The Birth of the Settlement

It is difficult to think of a less promising spot for what has become one of the world's major cities. Something must have been appealing about the marshy outlet of the River Amstel where it meets the River IJ (pronounced "Ay")—a tidal inlet of the Zuider Zee—even although the area flooded on a regular basis with water forced in by the prevailing winter winds.

The Batavians travelled down the Rhine to found the first permanent settlement here. Almost from the start the water had to be controlled, and the tradition of damming and organized diversion of the river and the tides began. It has been a constant source of concern ever since.

The settlement was entered on maps of the Roman Empire, but following Rome's decline, the land became the domain of various Germanic tribes in what is known throughout Europe as the "Dark Ages." This probably had little effect on the fledgling city, whose main trade was fishing.

Towards the end of the first millennium the land we now call the Netherlands was ruled by a number of feudal lords —assorted counts, dukes, and bishops who had total power over the land and the people who lived on it.

From Fishing to Trading

The first wooden houses were built in around 1200, on artificial mounds called *terps*. The town was fortified against rival lords, and against the seawater—the River Amstel being dammed at what is now Dam Square. This was not just to control the tides but also to manipulate trade, as it prevented seagoing ships from taking their goods down the river—they had to transfer the goods to locally owned boats for their journey. It gave the local populace a healthy income and began two important elements in the city's history, the predominance of the merchant classes and the use of barges for inland trade.

In 1275 the settlement of Amstelredamme, as it was known, received permission from Count Floris of Holland to transport goods along the river Amstel without incurring tolls, giving the city a monopoly on trade along the river. In 1323 Amstelredamme became a toll-free port for beer, and once a method of preserving herring had been perfected in the late 14th century, the town also had a product with a high profit margin and began exporting fish around Europe.

However, something happened in 1345 which caused Amstelredamme to change from being a mere trading port to a settlement of spiritual importance. A dying man was given a piece of communion bread which he could not swallow. When attendants threw the piece in the fire it would not burn. The event was declared a miracle and within a few years Amstelredamme became a place of pilgrimage, further increasing the wealth flowing into the city.

The early 15th century saw a healthy expansion of trade and the population rose dra-

A Delft depiction of William of Orange. His mark on Dutch history is indelible.

matically. Catastrophic fires destroyed a large part of the city in 1421 and again in 1452. Following the second fire, legislation made it illegal to build with wood, and brick became the material of choice. Today, only a few buildings remain from before the fires; the wooden Het Houten Huis in the Begijnhof is considered the oldest. The legislation brought about a veritable feast of civil engineering projects including the building of the city wall, incorporating the Waag and Shreierstoren, in around 1480.

The Arrival of the Spanish

Meanwhile, politically, the climate was changing with a series of dynastic inter-marriages. Philip of Burgundy began to bring some semblance of unification to the Low Countries (the region which roughly translates to the Netherlands and Belgium) in the 1420s. He was succeeded by Charles the Bold, whose daughter Maria married into the House of Hapsburg. Her son Philip married Isabella of Spain and in 1500 she gave birth to Charles, future Charles V, ruler of the Netherlands, Holy Roman Emperor, but more importantly, King of Spain and all her dominions—an empire on which it was said the sun never set.

Spanish rule was ruthless but, for a while, Amsterdam was left alone. Its position as an important trading post kept it apart from the more barbarous behavior in other areas. It saw a threefold increase in its population as refugees flooded in from other parts of the empire. Diamond polishers from Antwerp and Jews from Portugal brought their influences to the city.

Religious Strife

Amsterdam was already developing a reputation of tolerance as these new and disparate groups settled into the city. At the same time, Martin Luther's new Christian doctrine, Protestantism, was spreading like wildfire across Europe. It took a firm foothold in the northern provinces of the Low Countries —with Amsterdam at its heart. It was at this time that Huguenots (French Protestants) came to Amsterdam to flee persecution in their own country.

To counter Protestantism the Catholic Spanish instigated the vicious and cruel force of Inquisition. In 1535 there were anti-papacy demonstrations in Dam Square and in 1550 an Edict of Blood was issued by the Spanish to hunt out the heretics. Thus began 80 years of civil strife in Amsterdam and the region of Holland.

It is difficult to understand why Charles V, who was born in and had strong family ties to The Low Countries, should treat the region with such harshness, however the dynasty power base was in Spain and emotion had no part in Empire-making. In 1567 he sent the Duke of Alva to enforce heavy taxes and military rule on Amsterdam.

Towards Independence

This atmosphere of intense fear and violence sowed the seeds of revolt. The House of Orange (with a power base around the small town in France) had claim to lands in the Low Countries, and one member, William the Silent, began to organize opposition to Spanish rule.

In 1578, the people of Amsterdam rose up against the papal forces and threw them from the city—a time known as the Alteration. Unfortunately, though, all thoughts of tolerance were forgotten, and the zeal with which the Inquisition sought out Protestants was turned on Catholic worshippers. Their churches were violated and they were forced to convert, or to worship in fearful secrecy.

In 1579, seven provinces north of the Rhine conclude the Treaty of Utrecht, releasing the suffocating grip of Spanish rule.

Although William was murdered in 1584, his sons continued his work, and in 1648 the Treaties of The Hague and Westphalia saw the creation of the independent State of the Netherlands, whose boundaries were very much as they are today.

The Coming of the Golden Age

As Spanish influence faded, the Dutch star began to rise. First, they drew up agreements with the Portuguese, who had themselves concluded trade treaties in the East making them the sole source of new goods such as spices and silks. Merchants from Amsterdam bought these goods and sold them in the north, making vast profits in the process.

The fabulous bell tower of the Koninklijk Palace, a splendid reminder of the Golden Age.

When the Spanish took Portugal in 1580, the Amsterdam merchants decided to go into the import business themselves, and in 1595 sent their first fleet to Asia. In 1602 the Dutch East India Company (VOC) was founded and it obtained a monopoly on all trade routes east of the Cape of Good Hope. It founded a headquarters in Batavia (now Jakarta) in Java and obtained a monopoly trade agreement with Japan in 1641. VOC ships under the command of Abel Tasman landed in Australia some 150 years before Captain Cook.

The Dutch also looked to the west, and in 1609 sent Englishman Henry Hudson to search for a route to China. In fact, he landed far from China and discovered the river which still bears his name—the Hudson; he also traded with the native peoples for the purchase of Manhattan Island and travelled to the Caribbean, taking several islands as Dutch colonies.

Dutch ships brought back goods not seen before in the western world. Strange and wonderful creatures, new fruits and vegetables, and crafts of immense beauty, and they were all traded at immense profit with the nations of Europe. The Netherlands entered the period called the "Golden Age," when the VOC was more powerful than many countries, and Amsterdam was at the heart of this vast trading Empire.

"The Kitchen Maid," a Vermeer masterpiece, recalls Holland's Golden Age of Fine Arts as well as commerce.

Rich merchants needed banks and a support infrastructure, which developed quickly in the city. People flooded in to take advantage of the new commercial opportunities, the population rose rapidly and the old medieval city simply could not cope. It was still very much within the boundaries set almost 150 years before. Plans were made for a series of new canals forming in a ring or girdle around the old medieval horseshoe—three in all, Herengracht, Keizersgracht, and Prinsengracht. The canal side lots were sold to the wealthy of the city who built the finest houses they could afford. The confidence of the city brought opportunities for the arts and the burgeoning sciences. The artists Rembrandt, Frans Hals, Vermeer, and Paulus Potter were all working in this era, their work much in demand by the merchant classes. At the same time the Guild of Surgeons was learning about the physiology of the body at their meeting place in the Waag, helped by Antonie van Leeuwenhoek who had invented the microscope.

Decline and Fall

Expansion quickly peaked however, and the European powers who had carved up the New World set about testing each other in dynastic conflicts and colonial rivalry. The English were the main rivals of the Dutch on the high seas, and there were several wars between the two in the 17th and 18th centuries. In 1665–1667 the Dutch sailed up the River Medway and sank the British fleet moored there.

The 18th century saw Amsterdam grow into the foremost financial center in the world, but the seeds of decline had already been planted. When the English colonies in New England rose up in revolt against the British, they found ready allies in the Dutch. From their colonies in the Caribbean they sent caches of arms and ammunition. The British were furious and went to war in 1780, destroying the Dutch navy and signaling a sudden decline in power and influence from which the Netherlands never recovered. Trade suffered to such an extent that in 1791 the VOC went into liquidation.

In the latter part of the century there were anti-Orange demonstrations by pro-French factions in the country, and in 1795 Napoleon Bonaparte took the Netherlands in his epic march across Europe. Under the yoke of another foreign power, and with trade at an all time low, the Golden Age was truly dead.

The Return of the House of Orange

Napoleon installed his brother Louis as King of Holland and he chose to take the fine Town Hall on Dam Square as his palace—now the Koninklijk Palace. But only four years later he fled the city after civil disturbances broke out when he raised taxes.

When Napoleon's bubble burst and French power began to wane, William of Orange emerged from exile and was proclaimed king in 1813. Amsterdam had to work its way out of economic decline, but throughout the 19th century the city grew steadily. Industrialization changed the city. With the building of the Central Station at the end of the century, Amsterdam turned its back on its seafaring past and looked towards the mechanical age for its future. The station was built over the old harbor wall and some of the oldest canals in the city center were filled in to allow better access to motorized vehicles. Dam Square was landlocked for the first time in its history. However, in the spirit of the Victorian Age, the philanthropic city fathers funded the building of several major museums and parks, along with instigating social reforms which created one of the first welfare states.

The 20th Century

The Netherlands stayed neutral in WWI and efforts in the first half of the century were concentrated on land reclamation which increased agricultural production and living space. The Zuider Zee was finally tamed with the building of a 19-mile dike, the Afsluitdijk, in the north. In the depression of the early 1930s there were several schemes to cut unemployment, including the creation of Amsterdam Bos—a park and woodland on the outskirts of the city.

The Dutch hoped to remain neutral at the outbreak of WWII, but the Germans had other ideas and occupied the Low Countries in 1940. The Dutch Royal family and Parliament escaped the enemy to set up court in London. Amsterdammers were horrified at the treatment of their Jewish neighbors and the dock workers staged a brave one-day strike to protest, but almost all the Jews were transported to concentration camps, never to return. In Prinsengracht, Otto Frank and his family hid in the attic of their business premises for over two years before being discovered. His daughter Anne wrote a diary during their time in the attic, which became an international bestseller after the war. Anne her-

In charming Volendam, 17th-century architecture is perfectly preserved.

An ornate 17th-century gable reveals the high style and grandeur of a bygone era.

self died at a concentration camp only weeks before the war ended.

In September 1944, Operation Market Garden, made famous in the film *A Bridge Too Far*, saw thousands of allied paratroops dropping into the Netherlands to try and take key bridges on rivers leading to Germany. The people welcomed them and rose up to help them but the operation failed and the Germans punished the Dutch people during the winter of 1944–1945. Food and fuel were withdrawn, leaving the population to starve.

The Modern State

Soon after the end of the war, Dutch colonies in the Far East gained their independence—principally as the new country Indonesia—as Holland sought to rebuild its shattered infrastructure. The Dutch used this period to consolidate their social systems to the benefit of the whole community. Amsterdam became a mecca for counter-culture groups such as hippies, who were drawn by the well-known open-mindedness of the people.

"People power" began to exert its influence which ensured that, in Amsterdam at least, progress did not mean sweeping away the past. Where developers saw the opportunity to demolish derelict canal houses and warehouses, the people fought (sometimes literally) to save what they considered their heritage. Today much of the historic city is protected by statute although any redevelopment provokes much debate. The building of the Muziek Theater in the 1980s, which resulted in the demolition of several old houses, was a case in point—with vitriolic demonstrations by local pressure groups.

The Dutch embraced the European Union (EU)—they joined in 1957 when it was still called the European Community—seeing it as a way of increasing their security and their economic stability. Their natural strengths in agricultural production and trade have ensured their success in the new alliance, and the Netherlands has become an important base for foreign companies who have trade ties in Europe. Throughout the 1990s the Dutch have been at the forefront of a movement to open national borders, increase people's freedom of movement and expand trade within the EU, taking full part in the delicate negotiations which surrounded the launch of the Euro currency in 1999. Amsterdam has become one of the premier tourist cities in the world, trading on its historic center and its wealth of artistic collections. Today it operates very much as it did during the Golden Age with banking, trade, and modern "pilgrims" (in the form of tourists) to ensure that it remains a wealthy city.

Perhaps the only specter in the air is the one which worried the inhabitants of old Amstelredamme centuries before; water levels. Global warming over the next few decades threatens to raise water levels around the world, and the Netherlands— "nether" means "low-lying" or "below"—will have to work hard at solving the problem for its future inhabitants.

Historical Landmarks

c1200 The first wooden houses appear at the mouth of the Amstel.

c1250 The river Amstel is dammed.

1275 King Floris of Holland grants the settlement of Amstelredamme the rights to carry cargoes on the river toll-free.

1345 The "Miracle of Amsterdam."

1419 Philip of Burgundy rises to power, unifying the Low Countries.

1452 Fire destroys the wooden town. New buildings must be of brick or stone.

1516 Charles V heads the Spanish Empire and the Netherlands.

1535 Anti-papal demonstrations in Dam Square.

1567 Spanish military rule in Amsterdam.

1578 The Alteration—Protestants take control of Amsterdam.

1600–1700 The Golden Age for the Netherlands—an international Empire built with the Dutch East India Company at the center of trade with trading posts in the east. Canal building in Amsterdam. The arts reach a high with Rembrandt et al. producing excellent pieces.

1780 War with the English sees the Dutch Navy destroyed.

1791 The Dutch East India Company goes into liquidation.

1795 Napoleon takes the Netherlands.

1813 The House of Orange returns to power.

1889 Central Station opened.

1940 Neutral Netherlands invaded by German forces.

1944–1945 The Winter of Hunger.

1949 Indonesia gains Independence from Holland.

1960s "People power" saves parts of historic Amsterdam from redevelopment. Amsterdam becomes home to minority groups.

2002 Amsterdam celebrates the 400th anniversary of the founding of the Dutch East India Company. The Netherlands becomes the first country in the world to legalise regulated euthanasia.

WHERE TO GO

Amsterdam is a small city and eminently walkable, though if you only have a short time, take advantage of the tram system, which will transport you efficiently to all the most important attractions. Circle Tram 20 links them all on one route and runs at 10-minute intervals throughout the day from the central station.

Perhaps the most disconcerting thing for the newcomer is how to find your way around. The City center can seem at first like a maze of tiny streets and canals with no overall plan; however, in some ways it works very much like the plan of a spider's web and once you understand the structure of the town plan, it is relatively easy to get around. The central core, around Dam Square, is horseshoe-shaped, and consists of a series of wide streets — the main one is the Damrak/Rokin which cuts

> **When it comes to kisses on the cheek, four is the norm in the Netherlands — kiss each cheek twice, alternately.**

the center — and narrow alleys. It also has some of the oldest waterways, once so important for the delivery of goods from around the Dutch colonial world.

This area is ringed by a girdle of canals, the major ones are called *grachts*, running outward in ever larger circles. Singel was once the outer barrier for the medieval city, but as the city expanded, Herengracht (Gentleman's Canal), Keizersgracht (Emperor's Canal), and Prinsengracht (Princes' Canal) enlarged the web. Incidentally, if you do feel lost or confused when strolling, remember that these three canals are set in alphabetical order: H, K, and P.

Small streets (*straats*) radiate out from the center, crossing the canals by means of the thousands of bridges, which are such a distinctive part of the city landscape. To the north of the city center — the IJ becomes the IJsselmeer (a former route to the North Sea, now dammed); west of the IJ at this point is the Noordzeekanal — Amsterdam's present-day route to the open sea.

We have divided the city into four sections which are easy to follow on foot. We have started in the center of the city, where you will be able to take your bearings, obtain whatever information you need from the VVV Tourist information office, and take a **canal boat tour**. This is one of the most exciting ways to get an overview of historic Amsterdam and to see the true beauty of the city.

THE CENTER

Central Amsterdam — what was once the Medieval city —

is very small indeed. The port was the lifeblood of the city at that time and ships would sail right into the heart of Amstelredamme, as it was then known. Today, only a few architectural gems are left to remind us of this era, but the tangle of narrow alleyways gives a feel of the hustle and bustle which must have accompanied the traders.

The decision to locate the **Central Station** on the

Sint Nicolaaskerk and the Voorburgval canal bridge in the center of town.

site of the old harbor wall was the final death knell of maritime trade for the city. It stopped large cargo ships from landing their catches and diminished the importance of the canal systems. The station, opened in 1889, dominates the view up Damrak. The impressive building was designed by PJH Cuypers, who was also responsible for the design of the Rijksmuseum, and sits on three artificial islands supported by 8,687 wooden piles.

Across the wide **Stationplein** in front of the entrance you will find a large **VVV Amsterdam Tourist Office** where you can get information, buy transport tickets, make hotel reservations or book theater tickets. The office is housed in the rebuilt Noord Zuid Koffiehuis which was rebuilt in 1981 from the plans of the original. This was demolished when the metro was constructed in 1911. You will also find canal tour boats moored here, and thousands of bicycles waiting for their riders.

Walk over the square towards the city and, as you cross the canal bridge, look to your left to see the distinctive spires of **Sint Nicolaaskerk** (Saint Nicholas Church). Sint Nicolaas is an important saint for Amsterdam, being patron of the city and of seafarers. This Catholic Church replaced many of the secret chapels which were built for worship during the period of Catholic persecution and was completed in 1887.

Sint Nicolaas Day

Sint Nicolaas is the Patron Saint of sailors and also patron of Amsterdam itself. But perhaps most important, when he returns to the Netherlands at the end of every year he brings gifts for the children. *Sinterklaasvond* (Santa Claus Day) on December 5 is the date on which Dutch children traditionally receive their Christmas gifts.

A canal cruise boat on the Damrak, with a line of typical gabled Dutch buildings forming the backdrop.

Once over the bridge you will find yourself on **Damrak**. This wide boulevard was formerly a major docking area for sailing boats from the colonies. On your left you will find the marina area full of glass-topped tour boats. To your right, the street side is lined with fast food cafés giving it a slightly down at the heels appearance.

Just beyond the tour boats, at the head of Damrak is the **Beurs van Berlage**, the old stock exchange. Its refined modern lines were a revelation when it opened in 1903 and excited much debate in the city. Unfortunately it didn't excite traders quite as much and is now used as a concert and exhibition hall featuring everything from chamber music to modern art.

The warren of streets to the left of the Beurs building, is what Amsterdammers call *Oude Zijd* or Old Side, and this area constituted the old warehouse district in medieval times. The narrow alleyways are darker than in more modern parts of the city and the houses appear even narrower and taller. Dominating the streets is the imposing Gothic basilica of **Oude Kerk** (Old Church).

As its name suggests, Oude Kerk is the earliest Parish church in Amsterdam; work began on it at the start of the 13th century when Amstelredamme was only just starting as a trading town. Over the following three centuries, the church saw several extensions as the population of the city grew, until it took on the interesting and rather over-busy shape it is today — with several chapels adding gables to the original structure. In its early life it was more than a church, acting as a marketplace and hostel for the poor and needy.

> A serving of *genever* will always reach to the very rim of the glass. Bend down to the glass to sip the first mouthful to avoid spilling. Traditionally you should also be standing, and have your hands behind your back.

Once inside, the sheer scale of the church is immediate and impressive. Commemorative tombstones cover the floor, including that of Saskia, Rembrandt's wife. The stained glass windows are also impressive. One commemorates the Peace of Munster and shows a Spanish official handing over the charter recognizing the independent Dutch State. Several of the windows show Bible scenes on a majestic scale, but look also for the simple red door above which is written the advice "marry in haste, repent at leisure."

The canalside streets of Oudezijds Voorburgwal and Oudezijds Achterburg southwest of Oude Kerk are home to the infamous Amsterdam **Red Light District,** known to Amsterdammers as the *Walletjes* or "little walls." As with any large port, prostitution was rife from the earliest times, and although the Calvinist Protestants tried to stamp it out it has thrived to the present day. What makes the situation different in Amsterdam in modern times is that the industry has been legitimized and regulated in an attempt to curb the most disturbing facets of exploitation and in order to address health concerns. The prostitutes are entitled to regular health checks and are expected to pay taxes on their earnings — yet another example of the Dutch people's trademark pragmatic approach when it comes to tackling society's difficult issues. The area is safe — except perhaps in the early hours of the morning — and filled with tourists. The tree-lined canals and old narrow iron bridges are some of the prettiest in the city, and prostitutes ply their trade behind relatively discreet windows, not on the streets.

> Amsterdammers are friendly people. You may find them engaging you in conversation at bars or cafés as if you were old friends. This should be considered quite a normal and enjoyable part of your trip.

At ground level, seedy or amusing (depending on your point of view) shops sell sex wares, attracting customers from all walks of life; but don't get too distracted, else you'll miss the rows of dainty gables, quirky wall plaques, and window boxes brimming with flowers, which give the whole area a cheery feel. Don't be surprised to find offices, shops, and restaurants living side by side with the brothels here — it's all part of Amsterdam life.

At night the streets come alive with bars, clubs, and adult shows. It is one of liveliest parts of the city after dark. Just make sure that you stay on the busier and well-lit thoroughfares as you make your way back to your hotel.

You will find several historical gems as you wander Walletjes. One of the narrow houses on Oudezijds Voorburgwal

— number 40 — has a wonderful secret to share. **Museum Amstrelkring** was a merchant's house bought by Catholic Jan Hartman in 1661. Following the Alteration in 1578 Catholics were not permitted to practice their religion, and Hartman — along with a number of other wealthy Catholics of the time — had a secret chapel built, where his family and friends could worship. Although they were common at the time, this is now the only secret chapel left in the city, and because of its location in the house is called "Our Lord in the Attic" or *Ons' Lieve Heer op Solder*. Over its years of use as a church, three surrounding houses were added to create extra space, and several of the other rooms are furnished in authentic 18th-century style. It is a fascinating glimpse of a very difficult time in Amsterdam's history, but it's not just a museum piece — the church is still used for weddings.

The infamous Red Light District has more than sex on offer. Many buildings of historic value can be found here.

Zuiderkerk as seen through the arch of a cantilevered lift bridge.

Southeast of Oude Kerk you will walk through the small Chinese Quarter to reach **Waag**. This is one of the oldest buildings in the city and was opened in 1488 as a city gate, marking the eastern boundary of the city along the new wall built after the disastrous fire in the 1450s. The numerous turrets and rounded tower give it the look of a fairytale castle but it has had a more colorful history. Public executions were held here in the 16th century with the condemned being kept in a small cell on the ground floor before they met their fate. From the early 17th century it became the weigh house (the name Waaggebouw means "weigh house") for cargoes entering or leaving the city down the Geldersekade Canal to its north. The upper-floor rooms were taken by various trades' guilds for their meetings, and for one — the Guild of Surgeons — it was used for practical medical research, including experiments with cadavers. Rembrandt created two canvasses for the Guild of Surgeons, which have become two of his most famous paintings. *The Anatomy Lesson of Dr Tulp* and *The Anatomy Lesson of Dr Diejman* both show scenes from guild activities at the Waag and were hung here on their completion.

In the early 19th century the weigh house closed and Waag had a number of less illustrious tenants; it even spent some time as a furniture store. It now houses a café/bar, so you can have a refreshment and admire the impressive Gothic interior at the same time.

Nieuwmarkt (New Market) surrounds the Waag and it is home to several different types of market throughout the week. If you walk to the north side of the Waag and look up the Gelderskade you will see a tower dominating the sky-line. This is **Schreierstoren**, also part of the new city wall of 1480. City scholars are divided as to the reason for the tower's name. Some say it comes from the word *schreien*

Good day–*Daag*.

which means "weeping" as it was a place where sailors' weeping wives came to wave their men off to sea. Other say that the name is a derivation of *scherpe,* which means "sharp" — denoting the towers position on a 90-degree bend in the wall.

From Waag walk down Sint Antoniesbreestraat, past modern apartment blocks built for the workers of the city in the 1970s. On your right you will see the ornate tower of **Zuiderkerk** (South Church). This church was the first place of worship to be built following the Reformation and was begun in 1603. Designed by Hendrick de Keyser, its lines were much admired by Sir Christopher Wren, architect of St. Paul's Cathedral in London. It was de-consecrated in 1929 and is now a community information center.

The end of Sint Antoniesbreestraat brings you to a tiny square with a wonderful view up the Oudeschans Canal to your left. You'll find an old house, now a small bar/café, in the foreground and, in the background, the tower of **Montelbaanstoren**. Built as part of a new outer defensive wall in 1512 it originally had a flat roof — the ornate peak giving it such panache was added by de Keyser later in 1606. Today it is used by the local Water Authority as an office building.

After pausing to take a photograph, cross the street to Jodenbreestraat (Jewish Broad Street) and the 3-story brick building with red shutters. This is **Museum Het Rembrandthuis** (Rembrandt's House), and was home to the great artist from 1639 to1660.

The painter bought the house as he rose in prestige and wealth. He created a studio on the top floor, where there was abundant natural light to illuminate his subjects, and space for him to teach his numerous pupils. He lived with his wife and infant son on the first floor. The whole house was restored in the late 1990s, including the studio and the painter's *kunstkamer* or cabinet, to re-create the early 1600s as faithfully as possible. Over 250 of the artist's etchings have been beautifully presented on the upper floors of the

---

Rembrandt's Treasures

Rembrandt had a great love of collecting rare or precious objects. This desire was, in the end, a part of his downfall, but his collection — now seen in its rightful place at Het Rembrandthuis — tells us much about Dutch society in the 1600s. Beautiful man-made items from the Dutch colonies grace the collection. They sit beside Roman and Greek sculpture which hark back to the classical era. A number of globes indicate the expansion of the known world in Rembrandt's time; seashells and strange stuffed beasts are testament to the wondrous new discoveries found in these far off lands. Etchings by Raphael, Titian, and Holbein, kept in heavy leather-bound books, show new visual styles in form and color. Inspiration was rich indeed for the people of 16th-century Amsterdam.

The Muziek Theater — home to the Netherlands Opera and the National Ballet — sits majestically on the Amstel River.

house. Unfortunately, Rembrandt was not able to live out his life in his home. His lack of financial acumen and love of expensive objects caused him to become bankrupt in 1656 and he had to sell all his possessions, including the house, in 1660.

Het Rembrandthuis has, as a neighbor, one of the most up to date attractions in the city. **The Holland Experience** offers an audio-visual tour of Holland — its landscapes and traditional activities. Ride through colorful bulb fields or across the *polders* (low-lying lands reclaimed from the sea) and rivers from the comfort of your seat, and all in 30 minutes.

SOUTHEAST

Running parallel to Jodenbreestraat on the left-hand side is **Waterlooplein**, named after the famous battle and home to the famous flea market of the same name. Every day you'll find an eclectic mix of second-hand crockery, clothes, and electrical equipment on sale, along with cotton clothes from India or Indonesia. The eastern end of the market square is dominated by the twin spires of **Mozes en Aäronkerk** (Moses and Aaron Church), a Catholic Church built in 1840 on the site of a secret chapel. The Old Testament figures of Moses and Aaron were found depicted on gable stones in the original building and were set into the wall of the new edifice. The fine towers are actually wood rather than stone. They were painted to match the sandstone walls in a 1990 restoration.

Waterlooplein — and its market — used to be much larger, but a massive building project begun in the early 1980s cut its size considerably. Protesters deplored the loss of several old canal houses fringing the square which constituted much of what was

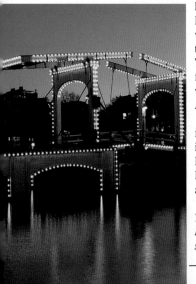

left of the old Jewish Quarter. Nevertheless, the construction went ahead, and the result of this labor is the **Muziek Theater** and **Stadhuis**, the front façade and entrance of which sits majestically on the Amstel River.

The attractive glass-fronted building was opened in 1986. It is home to the Netherlands Opera and the National Ballet and also hosts a range of traveling compa-

The Magere Brug (Skinny Bridge) with its arches and spars lit up at night.

nies in what is the largest auditorium in the Netherlands. Amsterdammers have christened this combination of town hall and theater the "stopera" (staduis+opera).

The **Amstel River** has always been a major artery through the city and even today you will see a large amount of commercial traffic passing along the waterway. From the terrace and walkway around the Muziek Theater there are wonderful views of the boats and the canal houses bordering the water. The bridge in front of Muziek Theater provides a wonderful view down the river and is also one of the most interesting bridges in Amsterdam. **Blauwbrug** (Blue Bridge) is named after the color of the previous bridge which occupied the site. The present bridge, dating from 1880, is based on Pont Alexander III in Paris and is ornamented with carvings of ships and other maritime themes.

Although Blauwbrug is the most ornate bridge in the city, Amsterdammers and visitors alike still have a soft spot for

---

Skinny or Misses Skinny?

How did Magere Brug get its name? *Mager* means "skinny" in Dutch and it would be simple to assume that the narrowness of the bridge gave it its name. Not so, say Amsterdammers who will regale you with stories of two sisters called Mager who had a house at either end of the bridge, or two sisters called Mager who paid for the original bridge to be built. By amazing coincidence, these two sisters were also extremely thin which prompts comments about the "*mager* Mager sisters."

Since the word *mager* is extremely difficult for non-Dutch speakers to pronounce authentically, one does wonder whether these stories may just be a way for Amsterdammers to poke a little friendly fun as we travelers tie our tongues in knots.

---

its neighbor just a little way south down the Amstel, **Magere Brug** or "Skinny Bridge." This white-painted wooden drawbridge is picture-perfect and one of the most enduring symbols of the city. It is even prettier at dusk when the lights on its arches and spars are switched on. There has been a bridge on this site since the 1670s but the present one was erected as recently as 1969.

Along the river on either side of Magere Brug are a number of wonderful barges moored on the banks. The huge craft which would once have carried heavy cargoes such as grain and coal now make surprisingly large, comfortable, quirky, and very expensive homes.

Beyond Magere Brug on the left bank of the Amstel you will see the façade of **Theater Carré**. Traditionally the site of the Carré Circus, the Carré family built a wooden structure on the site to house their shows. Later the structure was deemed to be a fire hazard and so they had this beautiful stone building

At the Museum Willet-Holthuysen you can see a furnished Golden Age home in perfect condition. Here, the kitchen.

Dutch Masters, Old and New

The Golden Age of the Netherlands history produced a number of brilliant artists who left a rich legacy of work in their country. In the years since, there have been further shining lights to grace the arts scene.

Frans Hals (c.1580–1666) is considered to be the founder of the Dutch School. His most famous portrait *The Laughing Cavalier* can be found in the Rijksmuseum.

Rembrandt Harmensz van Rijn (1606–1669). Today, the best known of The Dutch School (although some of his works are now thought to have been painted by his pupils) he revolutionized painting with his informal composition and use of light. He lived in Amsterdam for much of his life. Some of his best work can be found in the Rijksmuseum and a collection of his sketches at his house (Het Rembrandthuis).

Johannes (Jan) Vermeer (1632–1675) painted only around 30 paintings during his lifetime.His attention to detail and sympathetic use of light made his work famous. Vermeer's painting *The Kitchen Maid* can be found in the Rijksmuseum.

Jacob van Ruisdael (c.1628–1682). Master of the landscape, he has the ability to create an almost photographic realism. A number of his Dutch landscapes can be found in the Rijksmuseum.

Vincent van Gogh (1853–1890) began his working life apprenticed to an art dealer and discovered his own creative powers relatively late in life. His strong use of form and color developed after he settled in Provence. Suffering from mental disease, he died after shooting himself just before his revolutionary work was recognized. The Van Gogh Museum has over 200 of the painter's works.

Piet Mondrian (1872–1944) brought painting down to its essence with stark abstract lines and blocks created using primary colors. His work can be found in The Stedilijk Museum.

designed for them, which opened for performances in 1887. It now hosts many different types of performance, but a circus always appears here at Christmas time.

Cross the river via Magere Brug then travel one block north and take a left along the northern bank of the **Herengracht Canal**. Here you will get your first glimpse of the canal system which was built during Amsterdam's Golden Age and revolutionized the city. During its time, probably the most sought after and expensive real estate in the world. Herengracht particularly has many beautiful houses which can really only be appreciated by an afternoon strolling by them (see box page 66). This part of town is still mostly residential and many houses have been converted into apartments for successful Amsterdammers. It is fascinating to peek inside at the ultra-modern interiors, which give a feel of the flair the Dutch seem to have for interior design.

At number 605 Herengracht, **Museum Willet-Holthuysen** gives you the opportunity to look behind the façade of a genuine Golden Age house. It was completed in 1690 and structurally has been altered very little since that time, although it has been changed cosmetically several times as fashions

See you later–
Tot Ziens

changed. In 1855 it came into the possession of the Holthuysen family. Pieter Holthuysen was a successful trader in glass and English coal (which goes to prove that you didn't need to trade in exotic goods to become wealthy). After the death of Pieter and his wife, the house is bequeathed to their daughter Louisa who later married Abraham Willet. He had a love of art and was a founding member of the Royal Antiquarian Society — a society whose aim was to promote national art and history. On her death in 1895 Louisa bequeathed the house and its contents to the city of Amsterdam on condition that it would be opened as a museum. This it duly did in 1896. You will be able to examine in detail the furniture, porcelain, and numerous artworks collected by the family.

Travel further along Herengracht to the end of the second block. Here you will find one of the most fascinating views of the canal ring. From the bridge it is possible to see 14 other bridges by looking up and down Herengracht and ahead down the adjoining Reguliersgracht (this view is even better at water level, so take a canal cruise — and your camera!). Reguliersgracht has some very pretty houses and is quieter than the main three "girdle" canals built at this time.

The small square here is **Thorbeckeplein** and you will see a suitably somber statue of Johan Rudolf Thorbecke who designed the Dutch constitution in 1848. Wander through the square, which hosts an art market on Sundays, to reach **Rembrandtsplein**, one of the city's most vibrant social centers. Before 1878 this square was called Botermarkt, (a butter market was held here in the 19th century) but the square was renamed after the large statue of Rembrandt was sited here. One wonders what he

A statue of the old master standing watch over his square, Rembrandtsplein.

would have made of the square, for since the statue was unveiled, it has attracted theaters, cinemas, clubs, and show halls, along with a plethora of bars and restaurants and a curtain of vibrant neon signs all around the façade. On a summer evening it is one of the best places to sit with a drink and watch the world go by, and is within easy reach of a romantic walk along the canalsides.

Beyond the eastern end of Waterlooplein you will see the Visserplein, busy with several lanes of traffic. Head across the square to Weesperstraat to find the **Joods Historisch Museum** (Jewish Historical Museum) which documents the history of the once large and influential Jewish community in the city. Jewish history dates back to the late 16th century, but was cut short by the Nazi occupation of Amsterdam in 1940. The systematic deportation of the Jewish population to concentration camps destroyed the community and after the war only a handful of the thousands forced to leave returned to their homes.

> Amsterdammers will often take the aisle side of a double seat on trams and buses leaving the window seat empty; you'll need to address them directly in order to take the vacant seat.

The museum, which opened in 1987, was created by the amalgamation of four old Ashkanazi synagogue buildings. The exhibitions reveal the history of the Amsterdam Jews but also explain the philosophies of Judaism, and examine Jewish identity in a broader sense.

Across the busy road of Weesperstraat are two other reminders of the once-thriving Jewish community. In a stark, exposed position near the road in Jonas Daniël Meijerplein, is the **Dokwerker Statue** by Mari Andriessen. This figure of a true working man commemorates the day in February 1941 when the dock workers rose up in protest against the Nazi deportation of the Jews. Behind the statue is the **Portugese-Israëlitische Synagoge** (Portuguese Synagogue) which was inaugurated in 1675 for the Spanish and Portuguese Sephardic Jews who settled in the city. Its design is said to be based on that of King Solomon's Temple.

From Jonas Daniël Meijerplein look southeast to the glass houses of the **Hortus Botanicus** (Botanical Gardens) easily seen just across the Nieuwe Herengracht canal. Cross the canal by walking left along its banks to the nearby bridge. Once across, you have entered the Plantage area of the city, once an area of parkland but which developed from the mid-19th century into one of the first city suburbs.

The Botanical Gardens have a long and illustrious history. They began as a small medicinal garden in 1682, but soon became the depository for many of the new plant species

One of the distinctive glass house buildings of the Amsterdam's world-renowned Botanical Gardens.

brought from Dutch colonies in the Golden Age and were responsible for developing each genus for cultivation, propagation and commercial exploitation. The distinctive glass houses were added in 1912, and today the gardens have one of the largest collections in the world.

A two-minute walk down Plantage Middenlaan (Plantage Middle Road) leads you to **Artis**, a fascinating complex of zoo, aquarium, planetarium, and Geological Museum which aims to increase your knowledge of the physical world. The zoo was one of the first in Europe when it opened its doors in 1838, and it has continued as a groundbreaking institution, now acting as a center for efforts to save several endangered species of animals.

| Thank you– |
| Dank u |

Many of the old and confined Victorian enclosures where the animals were kept have been redeveloped in the 1990s to create more fitting environments for their majestic and healthy-looking animals. The Planetarium and other areas of Artis offer fun ways to learn about the world around us and are entertaining for adults and children alike.

Southeast of Artis, across two canals and busy roads, is **Oosterpark**, an open green area with a lake and play areas (we would suggest taking a tram — numbers 9 and 14 — rather than walking here from the city center). In the north-

---

Who cares about Sea Level?

Much of the land of North Holland has been reclaimed from the sea. This has been achieved by building a series of dikes and pumping the ground water to the far side of the dike to dry out the land. It may be difficult to believe, but many areas of western Amsterdam such as Vondelpark are 2.1 m (7 ft) below sea level and Schiphol Airport is 4.5 m (15 ft) below sea level. It's all testament to the ingenuity of man and the wonders of modern technology!

A little bit of Africa in Amsterdam — Zebras grazing in the savannah enclosure at Artis zoo.

ern corner of the park is the **Tropenmuseum**, once the home of the Dutch Colonial Institute. The building itself was built in 1926 and built especially to house the institute's collection of artifacts from the tropics. Today the aim of the museum is to improve our knowledge of the world's tropical areas, and promotes an understanding of the peoples in these developing parts of the world. A vast collection of artifacts from the former Dutch East Indies (now Indonesia) was the starting point for the displays, which range from tribal masks to tools and utensils in daily use. Recreations of a Bombay street and Arab souk, among other locales, bring home the reality of life in these very different societies. The museum also has a **Kindermuseum** (Children's Museum) offering 6–12 year olds a chance to explore the collection and interact with the exhibits. Special guides lead children through the artifacts and explain their context. The Kindermuseum must be booked in advance and at present the tours are in Dutch only.

North of Artis is **Entrepotdok**. In the 19th century this was the warehouse region of the city, and its carefully designed canals were one of the busiest port areas in Europe. The warehouses fell into disrepair in the 20th century, and lay empty for many years before they became a center for the 1960s and 1970s squatter revolution which overtook the city. Since the 1980s the area has been totally renovated, and

Clogs — not just footwear from yesteryear

Clogs and the Netherlands — mention one and the other immediately springs to mind. Many people would assume that clogs have been consigned to the pages of history, but it isn't so. Many people still wear them because they are as practical as they ever were.

Clogs are traditionally made from willow or poplar. These are popular trees for the river and polder banks because they can soak up as much as 1000 liters (264.2 gallons) of water per tree per day, keeping water levels under control.

Clogs are carved when the wood is freshly felled. After being shaped they are left to dry and harden. Clogs are traditionally worn two sizes larger than a person's shoe size. They are worn with thick socks, but should still fit loosely to avoid rubbing the skin of the feet. Only ceremonial clogs were painted; everyday pairs are simple and unadorned. You will often see farmers and sailors wearing them. Road workers and deliverymen also find them more comfortable than standard protective boots.

the warehouses gutted to create modern spacious housing, offices, and bars and restaurants without changing the basic design of the buildings.

Some inhabitants get a bird's eye view of Artis zoo — imagine looking out of your apartment window on a rainy Amsterdam day and seeing a small herd of grazing zebra.

Walk north through Entrepodok and you will reach the main route of Prinse Henrikkade which runs along the northern edge of the city (this would lead you back to central station if you turned left). Cross the bridge of the Nieuwe Vaart canal and walk towards a large square building with a masted sail ship docked outside. This is **The Scheepvaartmuseum** (The National Maritime Museum). As you cross the bridge, look left for a glimpse of the only windmill left in the city's central area. **The De Gooyer windmill** was built in the early part of the 18th century to grind corn.

The building housing The Scheepvaartmuseum was built in 1656 for the Dutch navy. Its strong walls safeguarded a vast arsenal used to protect Dutch interests around the known world. Today its extensive exhibits document the long and illustrious history of maritime achievement by the Dutch,

Pretty as a postcard — The restored 18th-century De Gooyer windmill.

Hop aboard this reproduction of "The Amsterdam," and take a trip back in time.

with paintings, maps, and maritime models explaining the part that ships — and particularly the VOC — played in the growth of the empire in the 17th century.

The Dutch Royal barge (last used in 1962) is also kept in air-conditioned splendor, but perhaps pride of place — and certainly what brings 18th-century seafaring to life — is the re-creation of a Dutch East India ship *The Amsterdam* which sits in the dock outside. She is the life-size replica of a real ship completed in 1748, but more than this, *The Amsterdam* has a "press-ganged" crew to man her. As you explore her decks, the captain will illustrate his course with charts of the time, the doctor will explain his rather primitive treatments, and the ordinary seamen will be happy to sing you a Dutch sea shanty.

Located next to the museum, and unmistakable by its modern shape and huge green outer walls, is the NEMO Science and Technology Center. Opened in 1997, the center was created to bring the latest science and technology literally into the hands of the lay person, whatever their age. Even the location of the building is a technological marvel. It sits high above the entrance to the IJ tunnel, which takes six lanes of traffic under the IJ waterway to Amsterdam's northern suburbs and north Holland beyond. Inside the center you can try your hand at playing the stock exchange by computer, change the wheel on a car, or look at the cells of the body through a microscope. There are hands-on experiments for everyone from young children to adults, focusing on five linked themes — Energy, Humanity, Interactivity, Science, and Technology.

SOUTHWEST

The southwest section takes on a fan shape from the center of the city, widening as it travels out and taking in the major art museums of the city.

Our starting point is **Muntplein**, at the junction of the Amstel and the Singel canals.

Although only a small square, and cut by so many tramlines that it is difficult to know which way to look, it has a very beautiful tower — **Muntorren** (Mint Tower). Originally a medieval gate guarding the entrance to the city, it was damaged by fire in 1619, and the clock tower was added by de Keyser during the renovations of 1620. In 1699 the carillon was installed and this still fills the air with its regular bell rounds. During the war with France in 1672, when Amsterdam had its supply of money cut off, the tower was transformed for a short time into the city mint, and the name has remained since that time.

> It will be difficult to find a no smoking area in bars and cafés. In summer nonsmokers would be wise to sit outside.

In the shadow of the tower, and floating on the Singel canal (the medieval protective moat for the city) is the **Bloemenmarkt** (Flower market). The daily market has been held for centuries, when the flower sellers would arrive by canal with boats laden with blooms. Today the stalls still float on the water but are permanently attached to the canal wall. The blooms they sell bring a splash of color to even the dullest Amsterdam day.

Stroll along the market until you reach Konigsplein and take a left down Leidsestraat. This is a major shopping street and one of the busiest because it links one of the largest squares in the city to the central area.

Stop at Metz and Co. department store, which sits on the corner of Keizersgracht and Leidsegracht. One of the oldest in town, it offers good views of the city from the café on the top floor.

At the end of Leidsestraat is **Leidseplein**, probably the busiest in the city and a major focus for "R&R" in the city. The bars and cafés spill out onto the square which strangely has no real point of focus, unlike Rembrandt-splein. Look out for a small grassy area, with sculptures of life-size iguanas and other large lizards. The narrow streets leading off the square are filled with cinemas, concert halls, and intimate live venues. There is also a busy VVV Amsterdam Tourist Office.

> Follow the locals in wearing casual, comfortable shoes. The city's uneven surfaces can be hard on the feet.

In summer you'll find several different street performers vying for your guilders. It's a place where talented music students play classical pieces, or musicians from around the world play their traditional tunes. In winter an ice rink fills the space so you can enjoy a skating session. Whatever the time of year, as the sun sets, the neon lights are switched on and people flock to enjoy the restaurants and nightclubs which keeps the square buzzing until the early hours of the morning.

On the western side of Leidseplein you will find the **Stadsschouwburg** (Municipal Theater) which was built in

1894. Once the premier opera house in the city, it has been usurped by the Muziek Theater, but still hosts regular performances of visiting and Dutch companies, being home to the Toneelgroep drama group. Next door sits the **American Hotel**, an Art Nouveau treasure and national monument completed in 1902. If you are not staying at the hotel be sure to visit the Café Americain on the first floor to enjoy the sumptuous surroundings, and perhaps share a coffee with a celebrity or two.

Street musicians keep things lively in Leidseplein, where there's always an audience.

Turn left once through Leidseplein and across the Singelgracht canal, and you will find the **Amsterdam Casino and Lido** on your left. On your right, across Stadhouderskade, is a narrow gate leading to **Vondelpark**. This park, founded in 1865, has been called "the lungs of Amsterdam" and was founded after a number of philanthropic city fathers decided that there was a need for a genteel recreation area for the city's population, many of whom lived in overcrowded slums. The park was named after the Netherlands' premier poet Joost van den Vondel and designed in the English fashion of the times. Today its 46 hectares (120 acres) have grazing farm animals, flocks of parakeets, jogging tracks, and cycle paths. The large pavilion, which opened in 1881, is now the **Nederlands Filmmuseum**. It shows more than 1000 films each year including outdoor screenings.

Only five minutes to the south of Leidseplein is the museum quarter, for many visitors the raison d'être for their visit to Amsterdam. Here, three of the most important art collections in Europe sit side by side, allowing visitors to walk from one to the next in a matter of moments. Although all very different in appearance, they are brought together by an open space which has recently been redesigned and replanted to accent the buildings. The square is called, not surprisingly, **Museumplein**.

The Rijksmuseum

 Pride of place must go to the **Rijksmuseum** (The National Art Gallery) with arguably the greatest collection of Dutch art in the world. However, most of the museum is due to close for renovation from late 2003 until 2008. One wing, the Philips Wing, should remain open for the display of key works in the collection, some of which are detailed below. To check on progress and to find out what is on show, visit the museum's website, <www.rijksmuseum.nl>.

The collection is housed in a magnificent Victorian Gothic building, which was designed by P. J. H. Cuypers and opened in 1885. The museum can be a confusing maze of connecting rooms — additions were completed in 1898 and 1919 — so it pays to sit down for a few minutes to study the very comprehensive map, which accompanies your ticket. A multimedia interactive study area also allows you to review the vast collection on a screen, pinpoint works that you want to see, and print out details of each piece. The center, called ARIA (Amsterdam Rijksmuseum InterActief), is located in room 225, behind the *Night Watch* room.

The magnificent Rijksmuseum, an architectural jewel and home to the greatest collection of Dutch art in the world.

The collection is varied but most visitors come to see the works of the Dutch masters. Dutch painting of the 15th to 17th centuries are to be found in rooms 201 to 236 on the second floor. Among the collection are 20 works by Rembrandt, including *The Nightwatch*, properly entitled *The Company of Captain Frans Banning Cocq and Lieutenant Willem van Ruytenburch*. The work, which was commissioned by the company for its barracks, is remarkable for its lack of formality and very different from the accepted style of the day.

Johannes Vermeer (1632–1675) is also well represented, and his effective use of light can be seen in *The Kitchen Maid*, painted in 1660 and now one of the gallery's best-loved pieces. There are paintings by Frans Hals, the founding artist of The Dutch School, along with a collection of Dutch artists influenced or schooled by the masters. Rembrandt was a prolific teacher and his pupils produced work so similar to his that in later years many were initially mistaken for the great artist's work.

Look out also for painting A17, by a lesser-known artist, Gerrit Adriaensz Berckheyde, which depicts Herengracht in 1672 when its grand houses were just being completed. The view has no trees and shows the "Gentleman's Canal" in pristine condition.

Pride of the Rijksmuseum — Rembrandt's "Night Watch" draws a veritable pilgrimage of admirers year round.

Works of later Dutch artists include a number by artists of The Hague School, which rose to fame in the late 1800s and whose best-known representative is Jan van Huysum.

The museum also has a collection of work by non-Dutch artists including Rubens, Tintoretto, and El Greco and impressive displays of porcelain, furniture, sculpture, and decorative arts including a large section of Asiatic art in the South Wing. It also has a restaurant for those who feel the need to take a break in the middle of their tour.

The Van Gogh Museum

Behind the ornate Gothic Rijksmuseum are the ultra-modern lines of the **Van Gogh Museum**, devoted to the work of this modern Dutch master. The main building was designed by Gerrit Reitveld and opened in 1973, however a large freestanding wing of circular design by Kisho Kurokawa was completed in 1999, to host temporary exhibitions.

The museum houses over 200 paintings and 500 drawings by the artist — one of the most infamous of the 19th century — and it constitutes the greatest collection of his work, covering all periods of his troubled career. The bulk of the

---

The Changing of The Nightwatch

The size of The Night Watch is impressive as you stand before it, yet amazingly the painting was originally even larger. The canvas was moved to the Dam Palace in 1715 but was too wide for the place chosen to display it; three figures originally at the right of the painting were therefore simply cut off to make the painting fit.

Originally, the painting showed the two major subjects entering the scene from the left. Now they stand central in the view, altering forever the original focus of Rembrandt's composition.

The Modernist simplicity of the Van Gogh Museum contrasts strikingly with the ornate Rijksmuseum.

collection was brought together by Theo Van Gogh, who also kept over 800 letters written by his brother, which, when read in conjunction with viewing the paintings, bring life and context to the works themselves.

Vincent's working life was short but frenetic, interspersed with periods of manic depression, and his paintings reflect his moods. His 1885 work *The Potato Eaters* shows the hard lives endured by the rural poor among whom Van Gogh lived at this time. Contrast this with the superb vibrant colors of *The Bedroom in Arles* and *Vase with Sunflowers*, both painted after Vincent moved to Provence in 1888. Van Gogh is renowned for his reinterpretation of the works of other artists, and the museum has prime examples of works based on paintings by Rembrandt, Delacroix, and Millet.

The Stedelijk Museum

Next door to the Van Gogh Museum is another, whose stately exterior presents a very different impression to its contents. The building of the **Stedelijk Museum** was finished in 1895. The façade is neolassical with figures of famous Dutch men such as the architect de Keyser gaze down on the passing crowds. It was built specifically to house the private art collection of Sophia de Bruyn, who then bequeathed it to the city in 1890. In 1938 it became the Museum of Modern Art, and today it displays a permanent range of work by celebrated artists and numerous temporary exhibitions which reflect the cutting edge in visual art genres such as photography and video. Look particularly for works by Marc Chagall, including his self portrait *Portrait of the Artist with Seven Fingers*, *Pregnant Woman,* and *Man with Violin*. Picasso is represented by several works, along with paintings by Monet, Cézanne, and Matisse. There is also a comprehensive examination of the De Stijl (The Style) art and design movement, which swept through the Netherlands in the post-WWI period. Gerrit Reitveld, designer of the Van Gogh Museum, has several designs in the collection, and the work of Piet Mondrian, the Dutch modernist, are some of the most popular in the museum.

> Do take care when walking on canalside routes. The cobbled roads are made even more uneven by the growth of tree roots which push the earth upwards.

If you feel exhausted after your "museum-fest," then the streets around the Museumplein offer some exciting retail therapy. Walk across Paulus Potterstraat from the Van Gogh Museum and you will find **Coster Diamonds**, one of the oldest "houses" in the city, where you can watch diamonds being polished and maybe buy a carat or two. Van Baerlstraat, bordering the west side of Museumplein, is the haute couture area of the city. For further culture of a musical nature the **Concertgebouw** on Van Bearlstraat is home to the orchestra of the same name. The main auditorium is considered to have almost perfect acoustics even though the designer of the building, Van Gendt, had no experience in this specialized area.

If you want to stroll back to town after your visit to the museums then walk through the open courtyard which cuts through the center of the Rijksmuseum, across Stadouderskade and on to the narrow street of **Nieuwe Speigalstraat**. This center of antique and art galleries has some wonderful windows to gaze into. Prices are said to be on the high side, but the dealers are some of the most experienced in the world and they are sure to give you good advice.

After art gazing, stop into a diamond house, and be dazzled further as a polisher shapes the treasured gemstones.

Walk north along the whole length of Nieuwe Speigalstraat and you will eventually reach Herengracht at its most spectacular point. When it was first dug, and the lots of land sold, it was soon realized that this section of the canal (between Vijzelstraat and Leidsestraat) would have the largest houses inhabited by the richest families in the city. For this reason it has become known as the **"Golden Bend."** Many of these buildings now house banks and financial institutions.

NORTHWEST

The northwest section abuts the center, commencing at **Kalverstraat**, the rather brash, "happening" shopping street which cuts the center of Amsterdam from north to south. When you reach **Spui** take a left into a small square — on Fridays you will find a book market here. On the north side of the square you will see a small alleyway which seems to lead between two houses. This is the entrance to the **Begijnhof**, a haven of peace in the center of the city.

The cluster of buildings around a small central square was set aside in 1346 for the benefit of Beguines, members of a lay Catholic sisterhood. They lived simple lives and in return for their lodgings undertook to care for the sick and educate the poor. Although nothing remains of the 14th-century

---

Amsterdam Pass

To make the most of your trip, the VVV has an Amsterdam Pass which has special vouchers giving free or reduced access to museums, canal cruises and public transport. You'll even get discounts on meals at certain restaurants in town. The one-day pass costs €26, the two-day pass €36 and the three-day pass €46. Passes can be bought through your travel agent before you travel to Amsterdam, otherwise from VVV.

houses, number 34 is **Het Houten Huis**, Amsterdam's oldest house, dating from 1488. The Catholic chapel dates from 1680 when it was built in a style to disguise its purpose. The stained glass windows depict the Miracle of Amsterdam. However, in the center of the courtyard is an earlier church now called the English Presbyterian Church. It was rented out to English and Scottish worshippers in 1607 following the Alteration, and the Pilgrim Fathers worshipped here before they set off on their long journey to the New World (they came to Amsterdam from England before they set sail for the New World).

The last Beguine died as recently as 1971 and today, although the houses are still offered only to single women of the Christian faith, the women are not expected to undertake lay work.

Behind the Begijnhof is the old Convent of St. Lucian, which became the city orphanage after the Alteration, although it was only open to well-to-do orphans; the poor had to fend for themselves. Extended several times, including a wing designed by de Keyser, it was opened as the **Amsterdam Historical Museum** in 1975 and its rooms reveal the details of the development of this fascinating city. You'll see plans, maps, and paintings depicting the streets

When is Holland not Holland?

Are we in the Netherlands or are we in Holland? Are the two terms interchangeable?

Well, no. To a Dutchman the word Holland doesn't mean the whole country — that's the Netherlands. The country is then split into 12 provinces of which North Holland and South Holland are two. Amsterdam is found in North Holland, hence all the publicity leaflets featuring the word 'Holland' and which contribute to the confusion.

With its ornate façade the Koninklijk Paleis dominates Dam Square, its pigeons, and people.

and canals as they were when just completed. The Golden Age is brought to life (rooms 5–15) but there is also an interesting section on 20th-century Amsterdam, the Nazi occupation, and efforts to protect and preserve the city. Tiny details, such as the relief above the Kalverstraat entrance which asks people to support the upkeep of the orphanage, also point to the museum's original purpose.

Once out of the museum, walk north. Take Kalverstraat, or if you find it a little too busy for comfort, take Rokin which runs parallel to Kalverstraat to the right. This wide street was once also a canal, which was drained and filled in to allow better access for modern forms of transport. On the far side of the canal you will see the elegant Georgian façade of the **Allard Pierson Museum**, the archaeological collection for the city. Another couple of minutes strolling will bring you to **Dam Square** (simply called Dam by Amsterdammers), the symbolic heart of the city.

Dam is a wide cobbled square, usually filled with people and pigeons, and dominated by the ornate façade of the **Koninklijk Paleis** (Royal Palace) which dates from 1655. It was originally built as the Town Hall, facing the landing wharfs of the Damrak, which would at that time have been busy with ships. The classical design, by Jacob van Campen gives some indication of the confidence of the city in the Golden Age — a statue of Atlas carrying the world on his shoulders sits astride the rear of the building, and in the sumptuous interior, only the best materials were used. When Louis Bonaparte, brother of Napoleon, became King of Holland in 1806, he demanded a

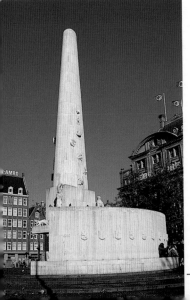

palace suitable for his position and requisitioned the Town Hall. He furnished it with the finest pieces of the time and left them all behind only four years later when he was forced out of power. It has remained a Royal Palace ever since but it is not a royal residence à la Buckingham Palace in London, and is only used for ceremonial occasions. It is possible to visit the palace in summer if there are no official activities taking place.

The National Monument in Dam Square commemorates Holland's role in WWII.

Beside the Palace sits **Nieuwe Kerk** (New Church) built before the Royal Palace, but not the oldest church in the city, hence its name. The church has suffered several catastrophic fires during its history and was stripped of all its treasures during the Alteration. The pulpit is interesting since it is beautiful but extremely ornate for a Protestant place of worship.

Across Dam Square is the stark, white **National Monument**, paid for by public subscription after WWII and erected in 1956. It commemorates the role of the Dutch nation in the war.

On Dam's south side you will find **Madame Tussauds**, a branch of the London waxworks. Not only will you be able to see figures of your favorite music and film stars here, along with a whole panorama which recreates Amsterdam's Golden Age, but also the windows on the upper floors give excellent views over the square.

> **Please–***Als tu blieft*
> **(often abbreviated
> to A.U.B. on notices
> and signs)**

Make your way behind the Royal Palace to Raadhuisstraat which will lead to the northern canal ring (Heren, Keizers, and Prinsen grachts). Immediately behind the palace is **Magna Plaza**, originally the main Post Office building built in 1899 in an almost exaggerated Gothic style. It was considered far too ornate for a civil service when it was originally opened but was refurbished — and the interior sympathetically adapted — in 1990 to house the city's only shopping mall.

Raadhuisstaat is the main thoroughfare to the north-western canal ring and is busy with trams, buses, and cars. It will take you quickly to the main attractions of the area but it is not the prettiest or quietest route. Wandering the smaller alleys and lanes to the north and south of it will be much more fulfilling (the details of the highlights of each

of the major canals can be seen on page 66). Follow
Raadhuisstraat until you reach the **Westerkerk**, set in its
own square on the left and overlooking Prinsengracht.
This church was designed by de Keyser in 1619 and was
one of his last commissions. It is said to be the burial place
of Rembrandt, but unfortunately no one knows knows the
exact location. One of his pupils Gerard de Lairesse painted the organ panels, which were added in 1686. In summer
you can climb the tower, the tallest in the city at 83m (273
ft), for incomparable views of the surrounding rooftops.
The crown on top of the bell tower is a replica of the
crown presented to the city in 1489 by Maximilian I, Holy
Roman Emperor.

Turn left beyond the church to Prinsengracht 263, just
an ordinary canal house-cum-office but made famous
worldwide by what happened here in WWII. This is **Anne
Frank Huis** (Anne Frank House), where during the Nazi
occupation of Amsterdam this young girl, her family, and
a small group of others hid for two years in an attempt to
avoid capture and deportation. Anne wrote a diary which
paints a clear and terrifying picture of the life the family

How did the postman make a delivery?

A formal system of addresses with street names and numbers was only introduced to the city in 1795. Before this,
gable stones and wall plaques were used as a way of indi-
cating either the purpose of a commercial building or to explain the precise site of a home — directions might have
been something like "three doors down from the Red Fox,"
or "next door to the writing hand." Many of these plaques
have been left in situ — look out for them as you stroll the
banks of the canals.

lived. It comes to an eerie stop only a few days before the family was discovered and sent to concentration camps. Of the eight people in hiding, only Anne's father survived — Anne died of typhus only weeks before the war ended — and after the war, in 1947, he published the diary. It became not only an international bestseller but also a symbol for the oppression of humankind.

The house, built in 1635, has been left much as it was at the time that Anne hid here. It opened as a museum in 1960. The secret rooms upstairs, where the family spent the daylight hours, are stark and bleak. A couple of magazine pin-ups still adorn one wall. The wooden bookcase, which hid the doorway to their refuge, is still *in situ*, propped open for visitors to climb the few stairs to their home.

Downstairs were the offices and warehouses of Mr Frank's business, which have been recreated in a multimillion dollar development opened in September 1999. Two adjacent buildings have been bought by the museum and refurbished, adding much-needed exhibition and audio-visual space, without compromis-

Canal houses and a boat make for a perfect photo op at Jonny Jordaanplein.

Hidden Treasures of the Canal Ring

The canal ring is made up of four concentric canals: Singel — once the outer defense of the medieval town — and Herengracht, Keizersgracht and Prinsengracht, built during Amsterdam's Golden Age. They run in parallel to each other, roughly along the western and southern side of the city in a girdle or ring known as the Grachtengordal. Here are some the interesting and unusual buildings to look out for as you stroll along the canalsides:

Singel

No. 7 is the narrowest house in the city.

No. 295 is still a brothel — only the huge lantern above the door gives the secret away.

The bridge at the junction of Oude Leliestraat has a jail built into it, recognizable by a iron-barred window.

Herengracht

No. 366. Two houses dating from 1662 now form the Bijbels Museum, which has a display of early, printed Bibles and archaeological finds.

No. 479 was built in 1665 for Jan Corver, Burgomaster of Amsterdam 19 times.

No. 502 is still the official residence of the Burgomaster (Lord Mayor) of Amsterdam.

No. 507 saw rioting and looting in 1696 when its owner and then Burgomaster Jacob Boreel instituted new taxes.

Keizersgracht (named after Holy Roman Emperor Maximilian I)

No. 123 is called the House of Six Heads because of the busts said to represent a group of six burglars caught and beheaded for their crimes.

Peter the Great stayed at No. 317, home of one of his best friends.

Look out for the narrow house at No. 345a. which almost seems to be squeezed between its two larger neighbors.

Numbers 353, 354, and 357 have pretty, matching gables dating from the early 18th century.

The artist Jacob de Wit lived in No. 385, until his death in 1754.

ing number 263 itself. You'll see videos of Anne's story and of Amsterdam under occupation along with photographs and artifacts of the time. Anne Frank Huis also acts as an education center and resource for political and philosophical groups fighting oppression in the present day.

Cross Prinsengracht to reach the area of the city known as the **Jordaan**. Built as housing for workers and artisans in the early 17th century it extends roughly from the far bank of Prinsengracht to Lijnbaansgracht, and from Brouwersgracht (Brewers Canal) in the north down to Leidseplein. Many of the streets were named after fragrant flowers but this was not the prettiest or sweetest smelling area of Amsterdam in its heyday. Overcrowding was rife, and with industries such as fabric-dyeing carried out on the ground floors, it was an unsanitary place to live. Its name is said to derive from the French word *jardin* since a large contingent of French Huguenots came to live here to escape political persecution in their homeland. Today, the Jordaan has been revived and it has become a fashionable residential area. You'll find many bars, restaurants, and interesting boutiques in the area. It's a good place to browse for an unusual souvenir of your trip.

THE OUTSKIRTS OF AMSTERDAM

Amsterdam is a large city despite its small center and the sprawling suburbs hold some attractions which you may find interesting.

Aviodome *(take the train to Schiphol Airport)*

Aviodome is the National Aeronautical Museum and is housed in a giant aluminium dome in the grounds of Schiphol Airport. It leads the visitor through the history of flight, from the Montgolfier Brothers and their balloons to the space race. Perhaps the most important part of the museum relates the history of KLM the national airline of the Netherlands, which is one of the oldest airline companies in the world.

Amsterdam Bos *(Bus numbers 170, 171, 172)*

The Netherlands suffered economic stagnation during the late 1920s and 1930s, as did most other developed countries. One of the methods used to relieve the problems of unemployment was to organize large community projects which were funded by the government. One of these was **Amsterdam Bos** or Amsterdam Wood, which created the largest recreation area in the city. In 1967 it was enlarged to its present 800 hectares (2,000 acres). Amsterdam Bos is more than a park. It has meadows, woodland, and a huge lake for rowing, sailing, and hourly row-boat hire. It features nature reserves, animal enclosures, and a botanical garden. There is also an open-air theater, which holds performances in the summer.

Zaanse Schans

Zaanse Schans is the archetypal Dutch landscape personified, and lies just a few miles north of Amsterdam center in the suburb of Zaadam.

This landscape is no accident or happy coincidence but a living museum created in 1960, which has brought together a number of farmhouses, windmills, dairies, and barns — real agricultural buildings which would have been demolished had they not been relocated here. Zaanse Schans has working mills, cheese-making factories, and clog workshops, situated on a canalside. You are free to explore at your own pace and maybe enjoy a *pannekoeken* (pancake) while you're there.

EXCURSIONS

A tour of the villages north of Amsterdam

Although Amsterdam is a city of 750,000 people, a ten-minute journey can transport you out into the countryside with fields as far as the eye can see. You don't need a car to visit and explore the pretty towns; public buses provide a very comprehensive, easy, and cheap service.

To the north of Amsterdam are several small towns which not only provide a contrast to the city landscape, but also take you to the heart of agricultural North Holland.

The landscape is flat, and cut with dikes and narrow drainage canals. Cows and sheep can be seen grazing, numerous wading birds, such as herons, keep a watchful eye

Named after the port it's moored in, the "Monnickendam" takes evident pride in its quaint home town.

The pretty village of Volendam, just one in a string of attractive towns that lie outside Amsterdam.

on the water, and every few hundred yards is a farmhouse complete with several single-story barns.

Broek in Waterland is the first settlement reached once outside the city environs. A small collection of quaint wooden houses it is surrounded by canals and natural streams. Further north is **Monnickendam**, once a large fishing port on the Zuider Zee which lost its raison d'être when the Afsluitdijk was completed in 1932.

The pretty gabled buildings which line the main street were once cottages for fisherfolk and the small port still plays host to a fleet of ships. Many are now in private hands, or work as pleasure boats in the summer season. There is also a large, private marina filled with sailboats which head out on to the open water on any sunny weekend. Walk around the old port to find vestiges of the traditional lifestyle. A few families still fish for eels, and process them in small "factories" along the quayside. In summer you can buy the catch of the day from stalls in the town. There are also some good fish restaurants around the harbor.

Just 5 km (2.75 miles) beyond Monnickendam is the community of **Marken**, one of the most beautiful villages in the Netherlands and home to a community of Calvinist Dutch whose traditions reach back hundreds of years. The older inhabitants of this close-knit community still wear traditional Dutch costume as everyday wear.

Until 1957 the village was situated on an island, remote from the outside world. The opening of a roadway linking the village to the mainland brought many changes for the inhabitants. Today Marken welcomes visitors but not their cars, which must be left in a large car park on the outskirts. You

> **Don't walk along cycle lanes! There is a possibility of serious injury.**

can walk through the village with its traditional painted wooden houses to the picture-perfect port. Stop at the tiny museum on the quayside, which holds an eclectic mix of seafaring and fishing memorabilia.

Traveling from Monnickendam to Marken, the road leads out into open water, home to hundreds of thousands of birds in the summer. The native herons, ducks, and moorhens see many species of migratory birds who fly north for the summer and return south as winter approaches. The road also makes for good cycling, being flat and smooth, or for walking. Head out towards the old lighthouse which sits surrounded by water on a lonely promontory.

North of Marken and Monnickendam is **Volendam**, a Catholic counterpart to the Protestant Marken. It is perhaps the village most changed by tourism, with cafés and souvenir shops lining the harbor.

Our tour finishes at the town of **Edam**, famed for its cheese, with a pretty *kaaswaag* (Cheese Weigh House) dating from 1592. Look out for the wonderfully named **Kwakelbrug** — the narrowest old bridge in town, which allows only single-file foot traffic to cross. The center of town has an unusual paved overlock, the **Damsluis,** just below the **Captain's House,** dating from 1540. Despite its worldwide renown, Edam is still unspoiled and there are some pretty restaurants where you can enjoy lunch before heading back to the city.

Haarlem and the Keukenhof bulb fields

Haarlem, situated only 19 km (12 miles) from Amsterdam is the birthplace of Frans Hals, father of The Dutch School of painting which developed during the Golden Age. He was a peer of Rembrandt's among others.

The center of town is a maze of narrow streets filled with historic buildings, all of which fall under the shadow of the 15th-century **St. Bavokerk**, an enormous Gothic edifice which boasts one of the finest organs in Europe installed in 1735. Mozart and Handel are both said to have played the instrument and you can hear it for yourself on Thursday afternoons in summer when recitals fill the church with music.

Across Lepelstraat from the church is the **Frans Hals Museum**, a suitable testimony to the town's most famous son, who was still happily painting in his eighties. The museum was opened in 1913 at the site of an old men's home and the **Vleeshal** (meat market) dating from 1603, both of which had been painted by Hals during his lifetime.

On the banks of the River Spaarne is **Teylers Museum**, founded by silk merchant Pieter Teyler van der Hulst in 1778, and said to be Holland's oldest public collection. Teyler, having no heir, bequeathed his fortune to the

A garden rainbow at Keukenhof. Here, narcissus and crocus preen alongside their more famous sibling, the tulip.

advancement of the arts and sciences, and there is an interesting collection of scientific instruments among other artifacts. The museum has collections ranging from minerals and fossils, to medals and coins.

Every spring from mid-April to the end of May, the fields between Haarlem and Amsterdam erupt in a rainbow of color, which stretches as far as the eye can see. The celebrated Dutch tulips flower in unison, creating a carpet as amazing as Joseph's Biblical coat, and they attract thousands of visitors for these few weeks of beauty.

Near the town of Lisse are the celebrated **Keukenhof Gardens**, a 28-hectare (69-acre) showpiece flower garden which opens its doors to the public. You'll find crocus, hyacinth, and narcissus blooms along with the tulip, in colors you nor-

A cheesemaker shows off her wares. In Holland's cheese towns, tradition is key.

mally only see in your imagination. The landscape at Keukenhof is enhanced by pretty windmills, adding to the authentic Dutch feel. There is also a restaurant and a gift shop where you can buy bulbs, blooms, and other Dutch souvenirs.

Nearby you can visit the **Bloemenveiling** or flower auction hall at Legmeerdijk. Every day it auctions millions of blooms, which disappear out of the auction room to be dispatched around the world within hours. It's fascinating to watch the action (or lack of it) as miniature trains carry the flowers through the auction hall for the buyers to assess. A large electronic bid-taker on the wall reflects the current bidding price; this happens several times every minute. The sheer size of the auction house is what gives pause for thought — the walkway for spectators is 1.6 km (1 mile) long.

Alkmaar and the cheese market

Dutch cheeses are world renowned, and the small red and yellow Edam and Gouda rounds can be found in supermarkets and grocery stores in just about every country of the western world. However in Holland, cheese isn't so much an industry as a way of life, and tradition still has a part to play in the production and distribution of the product.

Alkmaar is a small town 40 km (25 miles) from Amsterdam but easily reached by train or car. It has been the center of cheese production for many centuries and is now the only town which continues with a **cheese market** every Friday morning during the summer.

The large square in front of the 14th-century **Waaggebouw** or weigh house becomes a showcase of cheese. Rounds of cheese are piled there ready to be taken off on wooden sleds to be weighed. Uniformed teams of porters transport the sleds on shoulder harnesses and each team playfully attempts to be faster than their rivals, much to the amusement of the large crowd. The town enjoys a busy market for other produce on "cheese" Fridays.

The Waaggebouw contains the Hollandse Kaasmuseum or Holland Cheese museum, which is open throughout the summer, and, nearby, the **Grote Kerk** or Large Church contains the tomb of Floris V, who granted Amsterdam its rights to carry goods toll free in the 13th century. In a sense he started the economic life of the city and could be said to be its founding father.

Lean Times

As you stroll along the canalsides you'll notice that there are no houses which stand absolutely upright — in fact, some seem to stand at a very precarious angle indeed. Don't assume that the houses lean because of subsidence; most were designed to tilt towards the canal so that goods could be winched to the upper floors without crashing into the side of the house. Unfortunately some houses tilted too much, resulting in the 1565 building code which limited the lean to 1:25.

Highlights

Amsterdam is full of attractions, but here are the highlights — perhaps think of the list as a "best of the best" of Amsterdam.

Van Gogh Museum. More than 200 of the painter's works. Paulus Potterstraat 7, 1071 CX Amsterdam; Tel. 570 5200, fax 673 5053, <www.vangoghmuseum.nl>. Open daily 10am–5pm. Adults €7, children aged 13–18 €2.20.

Rijksmuseum. The collection includes many Dutch masters. Stadhouderskade 42, 1071 ZD Amsterdam; Tel. 673 2121, fax 679 8146, <www.rijksmuseum.nl>. Open daily 10am–5pm. €8.50 adults, under 19s free.

Stedelijk Museum of Modern Art. Paulus Potterstraat 13, 1071 CX Amsterdam; Tel. 573 2911, fax 675 2716, <www.stedelijk.nl>. Open daily 11am–5pm. Adults €5, children aged 7–16 €2.50.

Scheepvaartmuseum (the Netherlands Maritime Museum). Kattenburgerplein 1, 1018 KK Amsterdam; Tel. 523 2222, fax 523 2213, <www.scheepvaartmuseum.nl>. Open Tues–Sun 10am–5pm, Mon mid-June–mid-Sept 10am–5pm. Adults €7, children aged 6–17 €4.

Museum Amstelkring (the church in the attic). Oudezijds Voorburgwal 40, 1012 GE Amsterdam; Tel. 624 6604, fax 638 1822; e-mail <amstelkr@euronet.nl>. Open Mon–Sat 10am–5pm, Sun and public holidays 1pm–5pm. Adults €4.50, children €3.40.

Anne Frank Huis. Home of the young diarist who perished under Nazi rule. Prinsengracht 263, 1016 GV Amsterdam; Tel. 556 7100, fax 620 7999, <www.annefrank.nl>. Open daily 9am–5pm (April–August till 7pm). The museum is always busy in the afternoons — try to visit in the mornings if possible. Adults €6.40, children aged 10–17 €3.

Museum Willet-Holthuysen (furnished merchant's canal house). Herengracht 605, 1017 CE Amsterdam; Tel. 523 1833, fax 620 7789. Open Monday–Friday 10am–5pm, Saturday 11am–5pm. Adults €4, children aged 6–15 €2.

Amsterdams Historisch Museum (Amsterdam Historical Museum). Kalverstraat 92, 1012 PH Amsterdam; Tel. 523 1822, fax 620 7789, <www.ahm.nl>. Open Mon–Fri 10am–5pm, weekends 11am–5pm. Adults €6, children aged 6–15 €3.

Het Rembrandthuis (Rembrandt's House). Jodenbreesraat 4, 1011 NK Amsterdam; Tel. 520 0400, fax 520 0401, <www.rembrandthuis.nl>. Open Mon–Sat 10am–5pm, Sun 1pm–5pm. Adults €7, children aged 6–15 €1.50.

The Holland Experience multimedia show about Holland. Waterlooplein 17, 1011 NV Amsterdam; Tel. 422 2233, fax 422 2234, <www.holland-experience.nl>. Open Mon–Fri 9.30am–7pm (Oct–March 6pm). Adults €8, children aged 6–15 €7. The combined ticket includes admission to Rembrandt's House.

NEMO Science and Technology Center. Oosterdok 2, 1011 VX Amsterdam; Tel. 531 3233, fax 531 3535, <www.newmet.nl>. Open daily 10am–6pm, Satu 10am–9pm. Adults and children €9, children under 4 no charge.

Hortus Botanicus Botanical Garden. Plantage Middenlaan 2a, 1018 DD, Amsterdam; Tel. 625 8411, fax 625 7006, <www.hortus-botanicus.nl>. Open Mon–Fri 9am–5pm, weekends 11am–5pm (4pm October–March). Adults €5, children aged 5–14 €2.30.

Artis Zoo, Planetarium and Aquarium. Plantage Kerklaan 38-40, 1018 CZ Amsterdam; Tel. 523 3400, <www.artis.nl>. Open daily 9am–5pm, until 6pm in summer. Adults €13.50, children aged 4–11 €12.

WHAT TO DO

ENTERTAINMENT

It is said that there are over 40 different performances taking place on every evening of the year in Amsterdam. In other words, you will not be at a loss for things to do here. Concert halls and theaters are found all across the city with ballet, opera, pop performances, and classical orchestras all making regular contributions. There are also plenty of venues for more "risqué" or avant-garde performances.

The main venues for major performances are the Concertgebouw near Museumplein for orchestral and chamber concerts; Muziek Theater on the banks of the Amstel, which is home to the National Ballet and also holds performances of opera; Bimhius in Oude Schans —a Jazz/Blues venue; and the Koninklijk Theatre Carré near Magere Brug on the Amstel, which hosts musicals. If you would like to see stand-up comedy, Boom Chicago in Leidseplein, holds stand-up comedy performances in English.

You can book tickets for performances on your arrival but popular acts or plays may sell out quickly. The VVV issues a *What's on in Amsterdam* magazine on a monthly basis which lists the performances taking place each day. The easiest way to book tickets for performances before you arrive in town is through the Amsterdam Uit Bureau (AUB-Uitlijn). They produce a publication called *Culture in Amsterdam* with a listing of major performances. Contact them at Tel. 621 1211 and have your credit cards ready. Tickets can be posted to your home address or will be kept at the AUB office in Leidseplein for you to collect.

At any given time there will be temporary art exhibitions at galleries and museums around the city. The Film Museum in

Vondelpark also has special showings and film festivals. See *What's on in Amsterdam*.

The Holland Festival is a program of art events which take place all over the country throughout June. In Amsterdam the parks and *pleins* are filled with organized activities, and many galleries and concert halls hold coordinated events. A special ticket line will provide information about the festival activities, and tickets if you pay by credit card (Tel. 627 6566).

The Amsterdam Casino at Max Euweplein off Leidseplein offers the opportunity for adults to gamble (Tel. 620 1006). Open every day from 1:30pm.

A barman struts his stuff in the Drei Fleschjes, a genever tasting house.

There is no shortage of discos and nightclubs, particularly in the streets around Leidseplein and Rembrandtsplein—those in favor change by the month, so just follow the crowds if you want to find the most "happening" venue.

The Canals at Night

A night cruise along the canals with dinner is a wonderful and romantic way to get a different view of Amsterdam. Many of the bridges and historic buildings are lit at night, and the city is more peaceful. Lovers company (see page 116) has small and large boats and offers wine and cheese cruises or full dinner cruises. For a more private cruise (and one in which you can arrange your own itinerary) you can hire a water taxi in the smaller waterways.

SPORTS

Football (Soccer)

The Netherlands are football (soccer) crazy and Ajax is the Amsterdam team, one of the most successful in Europe over the last 30 years. They play at the Amsterdam Arena, a fine modern stadium, which is also used for other sporting events —but unfortunately it is almost impossible to obtain tickets for matches.

Whether it's serious or merely recreational, the Dutch love nothing more than to see the countryside on a bike. Join in!

*Take a leisurely paddle on a pedalo and see the
sights at your own speed.*

Amsterdam Parks

There are many wooded and park areas around the city
where it's possible to take a simple stroll or enjoy other outdoor activities. Amsterdam Bos (city woodland and recreational area), is the largest and most varied and offers a lake
for rowing, bridleways for horse rides, and tracks for cycling
—you could hire a bike and spend the day here. Many
Amsterdammers go running, frisbeeing, or simply take the
dog for a walk. The stables at Amsterdam Bos offer woodland rides, a perfect way to clear the city air from your system (contact Manege de Amsterdamse; Tel. 643 1432).

In summer locals enjoy an activity called "day camping" which means heading for an open space, erecting a

tent, and spending the day relaxing around it—perhaps with a barbecue. At the end of the day, they take the tent down and head home.

Watersports

With so much water around the city, it's not surprising that water-based sports are very popular. Even on the canals in the city center you'll find pedalos (sometimes called water cycles) to rent so that you can see the sights on your own steam. Contact them on Tel. 626 5574; fax 624 1033. You can also captain your own boat to explore the area. Canal Motorboats BV has two locations in the city; Tel. 422 7070 for information and reservations.

On the wider waterways outside the old part of town you will find rowing clubs and sailing clubs which take to the open water in good weather all year round. Out on the IJsselmeer (the inland waterway what was the Zuider Zee) on any sunny weekend you'll see hundreds of white sails breaking the horizon. Boats can be hired for trips out on the water from Monnikendam or you can take a trip on a crewed boat, although you'll need to make a booking well in advance. Contact Monnickendam Zeilcharters at 't Prooyen 4a, 1141 VD Monnickendam; Tel. 0299 652351; fax 0299 653618; e-mail <hzc@sailing.nl>.

Cycling

Despite spending more time than most people riding bicycles, cycling for fun is one of the major recreational activities of the Dutch. Cycle routes parallel most roadways making longer journeys relatively easy, and sporting groups or families will head out to villages like Monnikendam or Marken. Closer to the city, a ride through Vondelpark gives you a feeling of being out of the city. If you would like to tour with a group either in the city or surrounding countryside, you should contact Yellow Bike Guided Tours, Nieuwezijds Kolk 29; Tel. 620 6940, fax 620 7140. They operate daily tours with English guides between April and October.

Skating

Winter sports have traditionally played a big part in the lives of Amsterdammers and people from North Holland. When the rivers and canals freeze in winter, everyone is out skating—with long distance skating along the coast from town to town on cold, bright Sundays.

Not feeling sporty? Take a leisurely browse through the Waterlooplein market instead, and exercise your wallet.

Always on the market—Buy a bunch of blooms for now and a packet of bulbs for later.

SHOPPING

Where to Shop

Amsterdam is a gold mine for those who like to browse. The city has thankfully not yet been taken over by the international chain stores and the narrow streets of the center, the canal rings, and the Jordaan area are home to myriad small, independent boutiques—here you can wander for hours in search of that individual gift. The nearest street you have to "international" shopping, Kalverstraat, is home to the young fashion outlets and department stores.

Amsterdammers love to shop for their homes. Although many live in small apartments, what they lack in square footage they make up for in the quality of their environments, and interior design stores, or stores selling pretty household accessories feature in every shopping area.

The 9 Streets

The "**9 streets**" is a number of small alleys which form the ribs linking the Herengracht, Keizergracht, and Prinsengracht. Here you will find some very individual boutiques with imports from all over the world, as well as antiques shops and designer clothing shops. It's also a great place for small restaurants and bars.

For high-class fashions, stroll along PC Hooftstraat and Van Baerlestraat which border Museumplein. Although this "haute couture" quarter is small compared with that of Milan or Paris, you'll still find a good range to choose from, and stores feature work by both international and Dutch designers.

> **Items marked *Uitverkoop* are on sale.**

Markets

Amsterdam still has a good number of authentic street markets where you can mix with local people and pick up a bargain. Some markets cater to those with a specialist interest and are by no means a place to find inferior or cheap goods.

Perhaps the most famous market in Amsterdam is the **Bloemenmarkt** or flower market, which is held on the Singel everyday. As well as beautiful blooms you can buy bulbs and tubers to take home (if your customs authorities allow this).

The **flea market on Waterlooplein** also has an international reputation, although the market is much smaller since the building of the Muziek Theater. Many stall holders have moved to other locations in the city, although secondhand clothes still feature heavily, along with ethnic wear. It is open every day except Sunday.

Elandsgracht and Looiersgracht in the Jordaan both have a market for cheaper antiques, collectibles, and bric-a-brac. The stalls are found inside a number of old houses making it the perfect place to shop on a rainy day.

There is a **Boekenmarkt** (book market) every Friday on Spui in front of the entrance to the Begijnhof. Publications in various languages are on sale.

The **Kunstmarkt** or art market on Thorbeckeplein takes place on Sundays between March and November. This is a forum for independent artists in all genres and has work for many different tastes.

A summer **Antiekmarkt** or antique market meets at Nieuwmarkt on Sundays from May to September.

Postzegelmarkt–Nieuwezijds Voorburgwal. Stamp collectors every Wednesday and Saturday afternoon.

Albert Cuyperstraat is one of the largest general street markets in Europe. You'll be able to buy everything from fruit and vegetables to textiles.

Hedonists take note: Amsterdam has a small but excellent local cigar industry. Here, a purveyor of the finest tempts...

What to Buy

Antiques. The rich legacy of the Dutch colonial period makes Amsterdam one of the most interesting cities for antiques. European period furniture mixes with Southeast Asian artifacts, and art—there are dealers in almost every different specialist area. This is not a place for amateur collectors; prices are high but so is quality, the expertise of the dealers, and the advice which they give. Many of the finest shops are found around Nieuwe Spiegalstraat and the small streets leading from the Rijksmuseum back towards the city center, there are also a number on Rokin.

If you prefer the antiques of tomorrow there are also many stores full of "collectibles,"—most popular at present are turn-of-the-century light fittings, taps, and door furniture. (see Markets below). The VVV has a leaflet entitled *Spiegalwater—Arts and Antiques in Amsterdam* with a list of specialist dealers with their addresses and telephone numbers.

Art. The lure of the city for creative people has existed for centuries and modern artists follow in the wake of Rembrandt and the Dutch masters. Dozens of small galleries offer everything from classical to pop art. Exhibitions at the major galleries also promote the work of up and coming younger artists as well as established names. Street art is also very much in evidence especially in the summer. For those who enjoy the literal form of art, paintings and prints of windmills or canal houses can be found all across the city.

Diamonds. Before WWII, Amsterdam was a major center for the buying and polishing of diamonds. The industry was decimated by the loss of many Jewish families who ran the major diamond houses, but a slow recovery ensured its survival.

Today the industry is known for the quality of its polishing and of the expertise of many independent traders. Five main diamond houses are responsible for buying and polishing stones. They sell to smaller dealers but also sell to the public. You'll be able to see diamond polishers at work before you buy. You can choose from loose stones or finished pieces of jewelry. There are five main diamond houses in the city: Amsterdam Diamond Centre on Rokin (corner Dam), Coster Diamonds on Paulus Potterstraat facing Museumplein, Gassan Diamonds on Nieuwe Uilenburgerstraat, Van Moppes on Albert Cuyperstraat, and Stoeltie Diamonds on Wagenstraat.

Plants. The Netherlands are famed world-wide for their flowers and particularly the beautiful spring displays in the fields to the west of Amsterdam. Yet blooms are produced all year in hothouses scattered across the countryside and can be purchased at the Bloemenmarkt on the Singel. In addition to fresh flowers you can also buy bulbs to take home. The streets of Amsterdam have many independent florists with imaginative ideas in fresh and dried flowers. Even if you don't buy, it will inspire you for your return home.

Cigars. There is a small but high-quality cigar industry in Holland with a wide choice in terms of size and price. P.G.C. Hajenius on Rokin has been producing their own brand of cigars and importing the best in the world for 170 years. They also have a smoking café if you want to sit and enjoy your cigar on the premises. Their shop, specially built for the company in 1915, has a beautiful Art-Deco interior.

Jenever. Only the Dutch produce this alcoholic drink, a kind of amalgam of English gin and German *schnaps*. It is bottled in very distinctive stone flagons which make wonderful sou-

*Shopping on Leidsestraat is always fun, as much for the
social interactions as the souvenir-hunting options.*

venirs—and excellent rustic candlesticks when you have
drunk the contents, if the interiors of a hundred "brown bars"
are to be believed.

Pewter. You'll find old pewter objects in the Amsterdam
Historical Museum and the Scheepvaart Museum. In the
Golden Age, it was used to make everyday utensils such as
mugs, plates, and kettles. Today it is fashioned into all kinds
of objects although larger pieces are expensive. You'll also
find antique pieces in dealers shops for an even higher price.

Silver. Modern silver is fashioned into a range of objects and
styles of jewelry. You'll also find lots of older pieces—not

quite antique but still exquisite—in collectibles shops around the town in the form of pretty spoons, ornate pill and snuff boxes, or letter openers.

Delftware. The pottery style we now know as Delft (after the city to the southeast of Amsterdam) was produced in potteries all across the country during the Golden Age. There was a famous factory in Prinsengracht in the 1600s, which produced many fine pieces. The blue and white finish is standard Delft and you will find it at many high class outlets with prices which match the quality. Small porcelain likenesses of canal houses look pretty in the windows of houses and

---

Calendar of Events.

February/March In the build-up to Lent there are parades and parties.

March the Amsterdam Art Week Festival, with performances of opera, ballet and theater.

30 April The Queen's official birthday. Local town and village fêtes. Amsterdam has a city-wide party.

June The Holland Festival (see page 79).

Last week in August Uitmarkt, a week of free music and theater performances.

September First Saturday of the month, a flower parade from Aalsmeer to Amsterdam and back. The Jordaan Festival is ten days long and begins on the second Friday of the month.

Mid-November Sinterklaas arrives from the North Pole and travels through the streets of Amsterdam.

5 December Sinterklaas's saint's day and *pakjesavond* or Parcels Night, where he delivers his gifts to the children.

---

hotels. You can buy several of these to make your own line of narrow gables.

Other Dutch souvenirs. Throughout the city you'll find a range of souvenirs which epitomize the Holland of the tourist brochures. Wooden clogs feature prominently, either plain or painted in bright colors. Windmills are found everywhere, on tea-towels, T-shirts, or fridge magnets so that when you go the fridge to take out a slice of Dutch cheese (Edam or Gouda) you'll be able to think back wistfully to your trip.

AMSTERDAM FOR CHILDREN

Although some cities can be dull for children, Amsterdam has many attractions and activities to keep younger visitors occupied.

Clog out with Holland's traditional shoe. No shortage of color combos to choose from!

Take them on a canal cruise—seeing a city from a different perspective is great fun and a great education.

Tram rides—although this is the normal method which most Amsterdammers use to get to and from work, it is an unusual transportation method for most of the rest of us. Children will love the new adventure.

Big shoes to fill—With all its adult activities, Amsterdam is also a kid-friendly city.

The wax works of Madame Tussauds will have all the latest stars of music and films, so they can try and guess who the figures are before reading the exhibit details.

At the Artis complex there is the chance to explore the aquarium, zoo, and planetarium. If looking at the solar system doesn't excite your child then getting close to tigers and elephants might.

The technology center at newMetropolis is for the child in all of us. Experiments with energy, looking at cells in the human body through a microscope, or playing some virtual reality games will inspire every visitor whatever their age.

The recreation of the Dutch trading ship at the Scheepvaart Museum with its staff playing the part of sailors, brings out the sense of adventure in children.

If you visit Amsterdam in early December children will enjoy the parade as Sinterklaas (Santa Claus) makes his visit to the city on 5 December. He parades through the streets on horseback.

Throughout the summer there are activities in the major parks and pleins. Street theater, face painting, and hands-on art shows will keep up their enthusiasm and interest.

EATING OUT

The Dutch national cuisine has a limited range of dishes, yet eating out in Amsterdam can be one of the highlights of the trip. The reason?—the over 50 nationalities which inhabit the city also bring their own unique culinary delights to Amsterdam's restaurants. You could stay in the city for over a month and not eat the same style of food twice. This offers you the ideal opportunity to try something new, and means you'll never get tired of eating out.

Amsterdam is a café society, and restaurants and bars form a lively part of the social scene. Restaurants can range from the very formal, to the informal, with prices to match.

Dutch Dishes

Traditional Dutch food is seasonal and based on whatever was harvested from the land or the sea, with light summer dishes and hearty, filling winter foods. Although arable farms

**Bon appétit–
*Eet smakelijk***

abound in the countryside meat dishes were not generally part of the Dutch cuisine. Fish and dairy produce were always much more prevalent.

The Dutch breakfast (*ontbijt*) is a hearty one. Slices of ham and cheese, and perhaps boiled eggs with various breads and jam or honey are accompanied by strong milky coffee.

For lunch the Dutch enjoy *pannekoeken*, pancakes thicker than the French crêpe and made fresh as you order them. You can have savory (eggs and bacon for instance) or sweet toppings with fruit, chocolate, and cream, or perhaps one of each. *Uitsmijter* is another interesting and popular lunch dish, more often served in Dutch homes than in cafés. It consists of a slice of bread toasted on one side on to which a slice of ham and a fried egg are added.

Broodjes or sandwiches are available everywhere with a bewildering range of fillings. The local ham and Dutch cheeses are probably the most authentic if you want to eat local, and the combination is delicious eaten hot in a *toastje* or toasted sandwich.

Frites or french fries are served and eaten at any time of day—you'll see the stalls in pleins or on street corners—thickly cut and served simply with a spoonful of thick mayonnaise, delicious!

Winter dishes are suitably warming and hearty. Start with a bowl of *erwtensoep*, a thick pea soup with chunks of hearty sausage. Served with heavy bread or pumpernickel, it constitutes a meal in itself. The other main type of soup is *bruine bonen soep* made with red kidney beans. This may then be followed by *stamppot*, a puree of potato and vegetables served with slices of thick smoked sausage or *worst*, or *hutspot*, made with beef. Kale, or cabbage is the most common vegetable to be mixed with the potato.

Fish

Fish has been a mainstay of the Dutch diet for many generations, and it is always fresh and bountiful. Try halibut (*heilbot*), cod (*kabeljauw*), or haddock (*schelvis*), all of which come from the North Sea off the Dutch west coast. Local oysters and mussels are especially good, or smoked eel which is a local delicacy.

A dish which harks back to the Calvinists, and which is lighter on the palate is a basic dish of plaice with vegetables, where the fish is simply grilled and served with butter. You'll also find freshwater fish, called "sweetwater" fish by the Dutch, from the canals and rivers.

The Dutch love raw herrings or roll mops. This small Atlantic fish comes close to the shores of the North Sea and is still caught in vast numbers. Preserved herring used to be one of the most important Dutch exports when it was salted and packed in wooden boxes. Today, the herring is cleaned and marinated before being rolled. You'll see roll mop stalls in summer, as often as you see *frite* stalls.

Cheese

Cheese is eaten at breakfast or lunch rather than with dinner. There are several types of cheese produced in Holland which have become famous around the world. Both Gouda and Edam, named after the towns where they are produced, are easily identifiable, being round in shape and covered in a red or yellow wax which keeps the cheese airtight, allowing

Outdoor canalside café dining is the perfect way to enjoy Amsterdam while experiencing it's culinary delights.

Cheese, cheese, glorious cheese! Infinite variety and the highest of quality are a sure bet in Holland.

them to be kept for many months. Traditionally they were stored in a cool larder and a large cheese could last a family several weeks.

Desserts

The Dutch don't have a very sweet tooth, although most cafés and restaurants will have *apfelkoeken* (apple cake) on the menu. You will also find *stroopwafels*, waffles doused with maple syrup, and *poffertjes* small, shell-shaped pieces of dough, fried until brown in butter and sugar.

Indonesian Cuisine

The expansion of Dutch interests during the Golden Age brought a wealth of new ingredients and flavorings from the Far East. This added interest to native dishes, such as the Dutch habit of sprinkling nutmeg on cooked vegetables, but also, over the centuries, the close ties with the lands of what is now Indonesia have created a second Dutch national dish —*rijsttafel* (literally translated as "rice table"). Rijsttafel is a Dutch invention; an interpretation of Indonesian cuisine— though often less spicy then the real thing—which became accepted both in the old

> If asked out to dinner by Dutch people the protocol is always to pay for your share of the meal. That's where the saying "going Dutch" comes from.

colonies and in The Netherlands as a meal in itself. It consists of a number of small spicy meat, fish, or vegetable dishes— up to 32 in total—and a communal serving of rice. Take a serving of rice and put it in the middle of the plate, then take small amounts of the spicy dishes and place them around the outside of the plate. The tastes of the small dishes balance one another in both taste, texture, and heat (spiciness) to excite the palate. The standard dishes which you will find are *babi* (pork), *daging bronkos* (roast meat in coconut milk) *goreng kering* (pimento and fish paste), or small skewers of meat (*satay*) with peanut sauce. Any dish which is labeled "sambal" is guaranteed to be hot (spicy), but hot dishes will be tempered with dishes such as cooling marinated fruits and vegetables. If you don't want a full rijsttafel try ordering *nasi rames*, a smaller selection of dishes with rice which make an ideal light lunch.

There are many Indonesian restaurants throughout the city which offer rijsttafel with 10, 15, or 20 dishes, and it is a good introduction to Indonesian cuisine if you have never tried it.

Savory or sweet, pannekoeken (pancakes) make for a delicious snack, dessert, or even a full meal.

Wander along a few of Amsterdam's streets and you will soon see that choice is the name of the game when it comes to eating out. If you want the best in French cuisine—and there are restaurants with Michelin stars here—then you will have no difficulty at all. Japanese restaurants abound for the best in *sushi* or *teppanyaki*. Even good old steak can be found in Argentinean, American, or Mexican style. Other European cuisines on offer are Spanish *tapas* bars or Greek *tavernas* and you need look only a little further afield to find Egyptian kitchens, Moroccan *couscous* houses, or South African bistros. All these are in addition to a fine selection of Italian and Chinese restaurants. Your trip to Amsterdam could prove to be culinary journey around the world.

Drinks

The Dutch love their bars. You'll find one on almost every street corner and they are warm, welcoming places where you can sit for hours, people-watch, and, when necessary, wait for it to stop raining. The staple place to socialize is the "brown bar," as much an institution as the pub is in Britain. So called because of their brown stained walls, low lighting, and smoky interiors, brown bars sell alcohol, coffee, and light snacks. They will also have a range of newspapers and magazines for you to enjoy (always with at least one in English) while you have your drink—it helps to promote the political and social discussions which Amsterdammers enjoy so much. Each bar has its own character, essentially based around the personality of the owner and the clientele. You'll soon find one that suits you, whether your taste is for a background of dusky jazz vocals or a blast of heavy rock. Bars generally open late morning or mid afternoon and close around 1 or 2 am. Often, if there are customers a good atmosphere a bar will stay open until the last leaves.

And what's lunch without a brew? Lucky for you, Holland's beers are first-rate.

Traditional Dutch bars have historically centered on two products. Beer is one and *jenever* (pronounced "yen-eyver") the other. At one time, distillers and brewers had tasting houses or *proeflokaal* for their products where buyers would convene to test the latest brews or compare vintages. Today, there are only a few of these remaining in the city and they always serve a range of other drinks, in addition to their traditional one.

De Drei Fleishes (The Three Bottles) on Gravenstraat (behind Nieuwe Kerk) is the major jenever tasting house in the city, and it has changed little in appearance since it was opened in 1650—although the distillery it used to serve was converted into a hotel in the 1980s. Here you will be

Ritual consumption—Patrons sample the jenever at a local tasting house.

able to try different types of jenever, the young (*jonge*) clear jenever will a slight attack in the palate, and the old (*oude*) mellower variety which has been aged in wooden casks which impart a slightly yellow color. Or perhaps try a fruit-flavored jenever.

In de Wildeman on Kolksteeg is a tasting house for beers, and its minimalist wood-paneled rooms impart something of the feeling of a religious experience to this drink, which has been so much a part of Amsterdam life since the 13th century. There are over 50 types of beer available on draft,

> **The announcement**
> *Koffie is klaar* **means**
> **"Coffee is ready."**

supplemented by nearly 100 different beers in bottles. You'll be able to undertake a beer tour of Europe if you have the stamina.

Dutch-produced beer is generally a *pils* variety slightly stronger than British or American beer. If you order beer by the glass it will come in a 33ml (1 oz.) size and will be served chilled, a very sensible size for quenching the thirst. The two fingers of froth which finishes your beer is traditional and is leveled with the top of the glass with a white plastic measure.

Most bars will have a range of both beer and jenever for you to try, or you can order wine, coffee, or soft drinks.

Coffee is the lifeblood of the city. The strong black short serving of fresh brew—and it must be fresh—is sold in cafés and bars all across the city. It always comes with a sweet biscuit. Do specify when you order if you will want it with cream. This will arrive in a separate container.

To help you order...

Could we have a table?	**Heeft u een tafel voor ons?**
Do you have a set menu?	**Heeft u een vast menu?**

I'd like a/an/some…   **Ik zou graag… willen hebben**

… and read the menu

aardbeien	strawberries	**kool**	cabbage
ananas	pineapple	**lamsvlees**	lamb
biefstuk	steak	**patates frites**	French fries
bloemkool	cauliflower	**perzik**	peach
citroen	lemon	**pruimen**	plums
ei(eren)	egg(s)	**rundvlees**	beef
forel	trout	**sinaasappel**	orange
frambozen	raspberries	**uien**	onions
gehaktbal	meatball	**uitsmijter**	ham, roast beef
kaas	cheese		or cheese, and
karbonade	chop		eggs on bread
kersen	cherries	**varkensvlees**	pork
kip	chicken	**verse paling**	fresh eel
konijn	rabbit	**worstje**	sausage

Marijuana and its limited acceptability in the city.

The Amsterdam authorities have accepted the consumption of marijuana in certain "coffee houses" in the city. By this policy they hope to separate the consumption of so-called soft drugs from hard and very addictive drugs. Whatever the merits of the argument, many tourists are concerned that they may inadvertently wander into one of these coffee shops when they would rather not.

Don't worry: Smoking "coffee shops" are easy to spot, having psychedelic paint schemes and impressions of "the weed" on the outside. They will also have names such as Smokey Joe's, or Bad Man Smokey.

HANDY TRAVEL TIPS

An A–Z Summary of Practical Information

Amsterdam

A

ACCOMMODATION (see also CAMPING, YOUTH HOSTELS, and the list of Recommended Hotels starting on page 129)

Amsterdam has a wide range of accommodations in all standards and price ranges and lodging is found in all areas of the city. Hotels are rated by stars from one to five with five being the best class. Most hotels will have rooms for single travelers. You will find them at 20–30% below the price for a double room. Prices are higher in the summer months and lower in winter. Service charge and tax are included in the rates.

Modern five-star hotels will have every convenience from hairdryers to mini-bars, although breakfast may not be included in the price. In the lower-class hotels breakfast is usually included.

Given the architectural style of the buildings in Amsterdam you will find many of the lower-class hotels will have steep and narrow staircases leading to the upper floors. If you have problems climbing stairs or have young children, make inquiries about facilities before you make a booking. You will also find that many of the old houses converted into hotels will have rooms of varying sizes and hence varying prices. Do make inquiries about the size of the room before making a firm booking.

The Tourist Information offices in your own country will be able to provide a list of hotels in each class and price bracket. The VVV (see page 127) offices in Amsterdam can also find and book accommodation for you if you arrive in the city without a reservation. This is not advisable during the summer or during European school vacations in the spring and fall (exact dates change each year but generally the end of May and end of October). You can book directly with the hotel concerned or through The Netherlands Reservation Centre (NRC) P.O. Box 458, 2260 MG Leidschendam; Tel. (070) 370 5705; fax 320 1654; web site <www.visitholland.com>.

The VVV also operates a "Winter in Amsterdam" program in alliance with various hotels. This offers a package of accommodations with discount vouchers, which could prove to be a good deal for people who travel early or late in the year.

Boarding houses and B&B rooms are also available throughout the city, although these will not usually have rooms with private facilities and are not bookable through the VVV.

If you would like to live as the Amsterdammers do while on your trip, Amsterdam House acts as an agent for a number of apartments and house boats which can be rented short or long term. They can be contacted at Amstel 176a, 1017 AE Amsterdam; Tel. 626 2577; fax 626 2987; web site <www.amsterdamhouse.com>.

AIRPORTS

Schiphol Airport, (general switchboard Tel. 06/350 4050; web site <www.schiphol.nl>) 15 miles from the city center, is one of the busiest and most modern in Europe. It acts as a gateway to Europe for many airlines in North America and the Pacific, but particularly from the old Dutch colonial areas of the Far East and South Africa. Its tax-free shopping is considered some of the best in the world.

Every 30 minutes a shuttle bus leaves the airport, making a stop at all the major hotels in the city. Tickets (€10) are sold in the arrivals hall. The bus will also transport you back to the airport at the end of your stay.

There is a rail connection from the airport to Amsterdam Central Station (and to other cities in The Netherlands and on to Brussels in Belgium). This Central Station connection runs 24 hours a day although there are fewer trains at night. The journey takes only 15 minutes.

B

BICYCLE RENTAL *(fietsverhuur)*
Amsterdam is one of the most bicycle friendly cities in the world and it's a great way to get around. You can hire bicycles at MacBike at Mr

Amsterdam

Visserplein near Waterlooplein, Tel. 620 0985 or Take-a-Bike at Stationplein 12, Tel. 624 8391. Try it for a day… or longer. If you want to take a tour by bicycle, Yellow Bike runs regular tours around the city or out into the countryside. Contact them at Nieuwezijds Kolk 29; Tel. 620 6940, fax 620 7140; web site <www.yellowbike.nl>.

However, don't get too carried away with the romance of it all. Riding a bicycle is a responsible and serious undertaking. Take extra care and watch out for trams, cars, and other bicycles. It is advisable to wear a crash helmet, though Amsterdammers don't. Also make sure that you are fully insured.

BUDGETING for YOUR TRIP

Airport transfer by bus: €10, by taxi €35, by train €2.90.

Accommodation for one night in a medium quality double room: €110–180.

Three course dinner for one excluding drinks (which can add considerably to the bill): €30–40 per person.

Strippenkaart, for unlimited travel on bus, tram, and metro €5.90. Three-day transport pass: €10.70 per person.

Bicycle Rental: €6 per day.

Car hire: per day for compact car from €50, for medium sized car €65.

Entrance to Rijksmuseum: €8.50, under 19s go free.

Daytime canal cruise: one hour duration €8.50.

Museum Boat day ticket: €13.50.

Dinner Cruise: around €70.

Flights to Amsterdam: From Britain, return flights average £125 + tax; from New York to Amsterdam specials start at $350 plus tax.

C

CAMPING

There are a number of campsites within a few minutes' travel of the city center. These are well run and open throughout the summer although they can fill up early so it is sensible to make a reservation. Camping Amsterdam Bos is in the large park area to the south of the city with a direct bus link to the central station; Tel. 641 6868, fax 640 2378. Vliegenbos Camping is located north across the IJ waterway.

CAR RENTAL/HIRE

Amsterdam is a compact city with exceptionally good public transport systems and roads which favor cycle traffic. Parking is expensive and difficult to find in the city center. Cars found along central canalsides and streets are wheel clamped automatically if they are found to be parked illegally or if they are parked overtime.

If you are planning to stay in the city then it may not be worth considering vehicle rental; however, for touring the countryside it would certainly be worthwhile.

Most of the major international rental firms are represented in Amsterdam. You will also find agencies at Schiphol airport if you want to pick up a car directly from the airport.

Avis: Tel. 430 9609.

Budget: Tel. Den Haag (070) 384 4385.

Hertz: Tel. 504 0554.

Drivers must be over 21 (23 for some agencies so check when making a reservation) and have held a full license for at least 12 months. National or international licenses must be shown at the time of renting. Collision damage waiver is available at extra cost but is well worth the peace of mind—but do check your own vehicle, household, or credit card insurance before traveling, as you may already be covered.

Amsterdam

Prices start from around €50 per day for a compact car; a five-door hatchback (with more room) from €65 per day. Prices rise in peak season and drop if you hire the vehicle for more than a couple of days.

I'd like to hire a car.	**Ik zou graag een auto willen huren.**
today/tomorrow	**vandaag/morgen**
for one day/week	**voor één dag/één week**
Please include full insurance.	**Met een all-risk verzekering, alstublieft.**

CLIMATE

The Netherlands has unpredictable weather patterns similar to those of Britain and characterized by cold, wet winters and warm, wet summers. You can, however, have wonderful sunny day at all times of year, and Amsterdammers will always hope for long periods of bright, cold winter spells which freeze the waterways for their favorite winter sport—ice skating. Unfortunately, this has been happening increasingly rarely over the last 50 years.

Figures shown below are averages for each month and can vary.

Average temperatures

	J	F	M	A	M	J	J	A	S	O	N	D
°C	7	8	11	13	16	18	20	21	17	14	11	8
°F	45	46	52	55	61	64	68	70	63	57	52	46

Rainfall is as follows (approximate conversions).

January	60mm/2.75 in	July	60mm/2.75 in
February	40mm/1.8 in	August	55mm/2 in
March	60mm/2.75in	September	75mm/3 in
April	40mm/1.8in	October	75mm/3 in
May	50mm/2 in	November	80mm/3.25 in
June	60mm/2.75 in	December	60mm/2.75 in

CLOTHING

Given the information about climate above, a trip to Amsterdam requires several different types of clothing even if one is traveling in summer when in theory it should be warm. A layering system is the best approach so that one can take off or add clothing as one heats up or cools down. A rainproof outer layer should be taken whatever time of year you travel, and an umbrella. In winter, a thick coat or jacket will keep you warm in cold spells when the wind can bite.

On warm summer days, shorts, T-shirts, light shirts, and slacks or light dresses make ideal clothing. However, always carry an extra layer just in case, and take a light sweater or jacket for the evenings. Comfortable shoes are a must for the daytime whatever time of year you travel.

Amsterdam is a notoriously casual city, but if you intend to eat at some of the finer restaurants, or visit the ballet or opera, a shirt and tie for men and "dressy" ensemble for ladies would be appropriate.

COMPLAINTS

In the first instance complaints should be taken up with the establishment concerned. If you are still dissatisfied then approach the VVV with complaints about hotels and restaurants and the Chamber of Commerce (Tel. 662 1375) for other trade matters. They should be able to advise you further.

CRIME and SAFETY

Amsterdam is statistically one of the safest cities in Europe yet reports still persist of certain types of crime against visitors, notably luggage theft and pickpocketing. Always keep a watch on your luggage, especially when transferring it at the airport, Central Station, or to and from your hotel. Never carry cash, credit card, or passports in back pockets or open purses (handbags). Always be aware of your belongings especially in the crowded squares and in the Red Light district. Carry them close to your body, in a body belt or inside a pocket with a zip. Always leave valuables in the hotel safe.

Amsterdam

As far as personal safety is concerned, after dark keep to well-lit major thoroughfares. You'll find that many Amsterdammers walk to social engagements in town, so unless you are very late you will be walking on streets with other people. If in doubt get a tram —they run late into the evening and there will probably be a stop very near your hotel. Otherwise, take a taxi.

If you rent a car or take your own vehicle do not leave anything in the car, even in the glove box or trunk—it would be wise to leave the glove box open to show thieves that there is nothing inside.

If you do find that you have had anything stolen report it immediately to the police.

A word on drugs: Despite having relaxed its attitude to drugs (consumption of marijuana is allowed in a number of "smoking cafés" in the city), the possession of any hard drugs is still a criminal offense.

CUSTOMS and ENTRY REQUIREMENTS

Citizens of the EU, US, Australia, and New Zealand can visit for up to three months on production of a valid passport. South African citizens need a visa; contact the Netherlands Consulate General in Cape Town, Tel. (021) 421 5660 for more details.

EU nationals can import or export limitless goods for personal use on which duty has been paid, although guidelines on certain goods are as follows: 800 cigarettes, 600 cigars, 10 liters of spirits, 110 liters of wine, 110 liters of beer.

Non-EU nationals or EU citizens traveling from non-EU countries can import tax-free goods to the following limits: 200 cigarettes or 50 cigars or 250g of tobacco, 1 liter of spirits or 2 liters of fortified wine or 2 liters of non-sparkling wine, 50g of perfume, 500g of coffee, 100g of tea.

If you are a non-EU resident (US, Canada, Australia, NZ, SA) you can receive a refund on the Value Added Tax paid on goods purchased to take home. To qualify for a refund you must spend more than f300 in one shop in one day. The goods must be exported out of the country within three months. You must have the purchases, receipt, and the refund check available for customs officials to view as you leave the country. For further information contact Global Refund Holland bv, Tel. (023) 524 1909; fax (023) 524 6164; web site <www.taxfree.se>.

 D

DRIVING

The Netherlands drives on the right.

On traffic circles give way to traffic from the right.

Road conditions are generally good in The Netherlands. Within Amsterdam itself the main thoroughfares are wide and in good condition. Canalside roads are narrow and generally open to traffic traveling in one direction (i.e., up one side of the canal and down the other side). This adds to the difficulty of navigating. Just remember to keep the canal to your left and you can be sure that you are traveling on the correct side of the road.

Speed limits in towns or built up areas 30 or 50 km/h (20 or 30 mph). On divided highways and freeways 120 km/h (75 mph) reduced to 100 km/h (62.5 mph) in wet weather.

Amsterdam has unique factors which drivers need to keep in mind:

Always be aware of cyclists. They have their own traffic signals and cycle paths but still are prone to ride without care and attention. Few use lights at night.

Trams have priority over all other forms of transport, so watch for them. They also have their own signals on major roads. Be aware that tram tracks become very slippery when wet, so increase your stopping distances.

You will find that many canalside roads have blind exits (they may be in dips for instance). Both cyclists and car drivers can pull out without warning.

Vehicles meeting on narrow canal bridges can cause problems. Road signs with arrows showing directional priority should be posted; if not, use good humor and common sense—and be prepared to reverse off the bridge to allow traffic to flow.

Amsterdam

Canalside roads and many other thoroughfares in the old part of the city can only accommodate one vehicle. This means that when delivery and garbage trucks make their stops, vehicles behind them can be held up for many minutes.

Documents required for car rental are a valid national license or international license. If you travel with your own car to The Netherlands you will need to carry your valid driver's license, registration document, or document of ownership, valid insurance, a red warning triangle in case of breakdown, and a relevant international country identification sticker on the back of your car.

Parking. Streetside and canalside parking is expensive and finding a parking space can take forever. Tickets are dispensed from machines found every 100 m (100 yards) or so. You'll need change to insert into the machines. Any cars found without a parking ticket or found to be out of time will be clamped and fined. There are large car parks opposite the Central Station (Parking Amsterdam Centraal) and near Leidseplein (Europark) both open 24 hours a day. Parking from around €2.50 per hour/€25 per day. You can pay by credit card in these car parks.

Gas and Oil. Gas (petrol) stations are plentiful both in the city and main roads, and motorways. Gas is expensive by US and Canadian standards, but slightly cheaper than the UK.

If you need help the Dutch Automobile Association (Tel. 06 0888) offers roadside assistance. If you rent a car do make sure you are given information about what to do in the event of a breakdown.

Road signs. International pictographs are in widespread use, but here are some other signs which you may find.

Doorgaand verkeer	Through traffic
Eenrichtingsverkeer	One-way traffic
Einde inhaalverbod	End of no-passing zone

Dutch	English
Fietsers	Cyclists
Filevorming	Bottleneck
Gevaarlijke bocht	Dangerous bend
Inhaalverbod	No overtaking (passing)
Let op …	Watch out for …
Omleiding	Diversion (Detour)
Parkeerverbod	No parking
Pas op …	Attention
Rechts houden	Keep right
Slecht wegdek	Bad road surface
Snelheid verminderen	Reduce speed
Uitrit	Exit
Verboden in te rijden	No entry for vehicles …
Verkeer over één rijbaan	Single-lane traffic
Voetgangers	Pedestrians
Wegomlegging	Diversion
Werk in uitvoering	Roadworks in progress
Zachte berm	Soft shoulders
(international) driving license	**(internationaal) rijbewijs**
car registration papers	**kentekenbewijs**
green card (insurance)	**groene kaart**
Are we on the right road for …?	**Is dit de goede weg naar …?**
Fill it up, please, with …	**Vol, graag, met …**
super	**super**
regular	**normaal**
Please check the oil/tires/battery.	**Wilt u de olie/banden/ accu controleren?**

Amsterdam

| I've broken down. | **Ik heb autopech.** |
| There's been an accident. | **Er is een ongeluk gebeurd.** |

Fluid measures

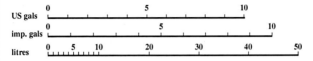

Distance

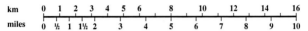

ELECTRICITY

The Netherlands operates on the 220 volt/50 cycle current. You will require an adapter for your electric appliances. The better hotels will be able to supply one to you.

American 110 volt appliances will require a transformer.

EMBASSIES/CONSULATES/HIGH COMMISSIONS

Although Amsterdam is the commercial and cultural capital of The Netherlands, the diplomatic and political capital is Den Haag (The Hague) and all the embassies have their offices there.

Australia: Carnegielaan 4, 2517 KD Den Haag; Tel. (070) 310 8200.

Canada: Sophialaan 7, 2514 JP Den Haag; Tel. (070) 311 1600.

New Zealand: Mauriskade 25, Den Haag; Tel. (070) 346 9324. Carnegielaan 10, 2517 KH Den Haag; Tel. as above.

Republic of Ireland: Doctor Kuyperstraat 9. 2514 BA Den Haag; Tel. (070) 363 0993.

South Africa: Wassenaarseweg 40, 2596 CJ Den Haag; Tel. (070) 392 4501.

UK: Lange Voorhout 10, 2514 ED Den Haag. Tel. (070) 364 5800. Consulate: Koningslaan 44. Amsterdam; Tel. 676 4343.

US: Lange Voorhout 102, 2514 EJ Den Haag. Tel. (070) 310 9209. Consulate: Museumplein 19. Amsterdam; Tel. 664 5661.

EMERGENCIES

For emergencies (fire, police, and accident) dial 112.

If you have a problem with theft or pickpocketing, there is a large police station at Lijbaansgracht 219; Tel. 559 2310.

G

GAY and LESBIAN TRAVELERS

Amsterdam is an extremely friendly city for gay and lesbian travelers. There are hotels which cater specifically for gay and lesbian travelers and a vibrant social scene, with clubs which operate for gays or lesbians only.

There is a Gay and Lesbian community center at Rozenstraat 14; Tel. 626 3087. The Gay and Lesbian Switchboard also has information about what's happening in the city (Tel. 623 6565).

GETTING THERE

By Air. Arrive at Amsterdam Schiphol airport, one of the largest and busiest in Europe. Most of the world major airlines operate flights to Schiphol but KLM, the national airline of The Netherlands, has a large network and flies direct to the US, Canada, South Africa, and Australia/New Zealand via Bangkok and Singapore. It also has airline partners such as Northwest Airlines in the US. For reservations contact KLM on Tel. 474 7747 in Schiphol, 800-447-4747 (toll-free in the US). Airlines which run nonstop services to Schiphol include TWA and United Airlines.

There are several flights daily from London airports, Manchester, and several regional UK airports to Schiphol. Flights take around one hour. British Airways and British Midland (KLM partner) both operate services.

By Sea. There are several ferry services from mainland Britain to The Netherlands. P&O/North Sea Ferries operates a daily 14-hour service from Hull to Rotterdam (Tel. 0990 707 070). There are also Stena Sealink sailings from Harwich to the Hook of Holland by car or train-boat-train in conjunction with British Rail and Dutch Railways (1482 377 177).

By Train. Travelers from Britain can use the Eurostar train service from London through the Channel Tunnel. For those who wish to visit Amsterdam as part of a European train "tour" there are special prices for monthly passes and special tickets prices for under 26s and over 65s. Further details can be found on the web site <www.eurorail.com>.

GUIDES and TOURS

There are a number of qualified English-speaking guides who offer tours of the city. Some have specialities, some take groups or will offer an individual service. Contact the VVV for a list of names and addresses.

A number of companies offer boat tours along the canals and these are probably the most popular activities in the city. Multilingual commentary keeps you informed about the attractions as you float along past them. Contact Rederij Lovers (Tel. 622 2181; fax 625 9301; web site <www.lovers.nl>) or simply head to Damrak and Stationplein where the boats depart.

Yellow Bike offer accompanied bicycle tours of the city with English-speaking guides. Contact them on Tel. 620 6940; fax 620 7140; web site <www.yellowbike.nl>.

HEALTH and MEDICAL CARE

The Netherlands is a modern and well run country and its medical facilities are just the same. There are no health concerns about the city, although mosquitoes can be a nuisance in the summer so anti-mosquito sprays or creams are useful (you will have no problem buying them in the city). You will not need innoculations to travel here. Most doctors and other medical professionals will speak good English. Many proprietary brands of drugs are available over the counter from pharmacies. Trained pharmacists (*apotheek*) will be able to give sound advice about medicines for minor ailments. Tel. 664 2111 to find out which pharmacists are open after hours and for the addresses of emergency doctors and dentists.

Always take out suitable travel insurance to cover any health problem you may have on your trip. You will be asked to pay for any medical treatment and should cover yourself against something serious happening to you.

EU citizens will be covered for medical treatment if carrying an E111 form filled out and endorsed by a post office prior to travel. They will need to pay for treatment at the time but will be able to claim a refund on return.

The water is safe to drink although most people prefer bottled water.

HOLIDAYS

The following dates are official holidays:

1 January	*Nieuwjaar*	New Years Day
30 April	*Koninginnedag*	The Queens Birthday
25 and 26 December	*Keerfest*	Christmas

Moveable dates are as follows:

Goede Vrijdag	Good Friday
Tweede Paasdag	Easter Monday
Hemelvaartsdag	Ascension Day
Tweede Pinksterdag	Whitsuntide

All shops are offices will be closed for all the above holidays.

L

LANGUAGE

There are around 30 million Dutch speakers in the world, with Afrikaans (South Africa) and Flemish (Vlaams) of Belgium being closely allied to it. Its structure similar to German but grammatically easier.

That said, the Dutch will usually speak English well and other languages passably and you will rarely need to resort to your language guide book. However, knowing and using a few words of the language of the country you are visiting is only polite, and it will gain you many friendly comments.

Do you speak English?	**Spreekt u Engels?**
Good morning	**Goede morgen**
Good afternoon	**Goede middag**
Good evening	**Goeden avond**
Please/Thank you	**Alstublieft/Dank u**
You're welcome	**Tot uw dienst**
Goodbye/See you later	**Dag/Tot ziens**

Useful Vocabulary (See cover flap for more useful expressions)

yesterday/today/tomorrow	**gisteren/vandaag/morgen**
day/week/month/year	**dag/week/maand/jaar**
left/right	**links/rechts**
large/small	**groot/klein**
old/new	**oud/nieuw**
up/down	**boven/beneden**
hot/cold	**warm/koud**
What does this mean?	**Wat betekent dit?**

Numbers

0	**nul**	10	**tien**	20	**twintig**

1	**een**	11	**elf**	21	**eenentwintig**
2	**twee**	12	**twaalf**	30	**dertig**
3	**drie**	13	**dertien**	40	**veertig**
4	**vier**	14	**veertien**	50	**vijftig**
5	**vijf**	15	**vijftien**	60	**zestig**
6	**zes**	16	**zestien**	70	**zeventig**
7	**zeven**	17	**zeventien**	80	**tachtig**
8	**acht**	18	**achttien**	90	**negentig**
9	**negen**	19	**negentien**	100	**honderd**

Days

Sunday	**zondag**	Thursday	**donderdag**
Monday	**maandag**	Friday	**vrijdag**
Tuesday	**dinsdag**	Saturday	**zaterdag**
Wednesday	**woensdag**		

LAUNDRY and DRY CLEANING

Most major hotels will organize laundry and dry cleaning services for you at a price premium. If you wish to organize your own cleaning, there is a central laundry/dry cleaners which is open seven days a week. Contact Clean Brothers Stomerij at Kerkstraat 56; Tel. 622 0273; they are open 7am–9pm.

M

MAPS

The Tourist Office or VVV (see page 127) produce several different maps, which could be of use to travelers.

The Tourist Guide to Public Transport in Amsterdam has a map with public transport services superimposed on the basic city map. There is also the *City Map Amsterdam*—a simple map showing the location of all the major attractions.

Amsterdam

For a very comprehensive map, Michelin's Amsterdam 1cm:150 m map covers both the city center and suburbs, with the city center expanded for ease of use.

MEDIA

Newspapers and magazines (*krant, tijdschrift*). Many English newspapers and magazines can be readily bought in the city. London papers will be there only a little after they are on sale at home. US papers will be a day old but the *Herald Tribune* publishes an International version in Paris which is published daily.

Most major hotels have a supply in their gift shops or at reception.

TV and Radio (*Televisie, radio*). The Netherlands has a number of Dutch television stations. Often they serve a local community. They also take services from various European countries including British stations. The Dutch use subtitles to translate foreign programs, rather than dubbing, so you will be able to understand the broadcasts (it is one reason why the Dutch are so adept at English and other languages). Most major hotels will have CNN; almost pick up the BBC.

The Netherlands has a generally good reception for BBC radio transmissions.

MONEY

MONEY MATTERS

In common with most other EU countries, the euro (EUR) is the official currency used in The Netherlands. Notes are denominated in 5, 10, 20, 50, 100 and 500 euros; coins in 1 and 2 euros and 1, 2, 5, 10, 20 and 50 cents.

Currency can be exchanged in public banks and bureaux de change, which can be found at the Central Station, Leidseplein, and in major shopping areas. Bureau de change offices are open longer hours than banks. There is a 24-hour exchange office in the Central Station. Exchange rates and commission fees will be posted in the windows of these establishments. Traveler's checks are accepted for commercial transactions and exchanged in the above establishments. You will need your passport to cash or use traveler's checks. There's an American Express located on the Damrak, and a Thomas Cook on the Dam.

International ATMs are common and will be indicated by the Cirrus or Plus signs on the machine. These machines also provide cash against Mastercard and Visa credit/debit cards.

Major credit cards are widely accepted in hotels, restaurants, and shops, although there may be a lower limit on payments in shops.

OPEN HOURS

Offices are generally open Monday–Friday 9am–5pm.

Banks are open from 9am–4pm Monday–Friday extended to 5pm for main branches. Late opening on Thursdays from 4:30pm–7pm.

The central post office at Singel 250 is open 8:30am–6pm (8:30pm on Thursday), Saturday 9am–3pm.

The VVV office on Stationplein is open daily. From September–Easter: Monday–Friday 9am–6pm, Saturday 9am–5pm, Sunday 10am–1pm and 2pm–5pm. From Easter–June: Monday–Saturday 9am–11pm, Sunday 9am–9pm. July and August, daily 8am–11pm.

Shops are generally open Tuesday–Saturday from 10am–6pm, 9pm on Thursday. Many shops extend their open hours in summer.

POLICE

Police headquarters (*hoofdbureau van politie*) is found on Elandsgracht 117, 1016 TT Amsterdam; Tel. 559 9111. There is a large police station at Lijbaansgracht 219; Tel. 559 2310.

The emergency number is 112.

You will also find work teams in the following central locations: Nieuwezijds Voorburgwal 104 (in the Red Light district).

Amsterdam

Nieuwemarkt Kiezerstraat (near Waag).

Prinsengracht 1109.

Police patrols take place in cars (see the word *politie* painted on the side) and on foot. Dutch police wear navy-blue uniforms. They carry firearms as a matter of course, but are approachable to answer basic problems such as "Can you point the way to the…?"

POST OFFICES

Post offices are distinguished by the PTT signs outside. They sell stamps and telegrams, change currency and traveler's checks. They also have fax and telephone services. The central post office is at Singel 250 and is open 8:30am–6pm (8:30pm on Thursday), Saturday 9am–3pm. It is always extremely busy and if you only want to purchase stamps, most shops where you buy postcards will also sell stamps.

For cheaper, quick communication, there is an internet café at Prinsengracht 480, which is open from noon–1am daily.

PUBLIC TRANSPORTATION

Public transport in Amsterdam and the surrounding area is excellent, with a comprehensive system running throughout the day and into the evening, and a limited service running throughout the night on key routes. Tickets are coordinated so that you can use them on buses, trams, and on the limited metro (or underground) services.

You will be given a "Tourist Guide to Public Transport in Amsterdam" leaflet with your ticket along with a leaflet about Circle-Tram 20, whose route links most of the major attractions in the city. This runs at 10-minute intervals on a clockwise and anti-clockwise route. If you intend to travel by bus at night (after midnight) then ask for the "Nightbus" leaflet which explains the routes and running times.

Trams are fun for those who don't use them every day, but do be aware of some special safety issues:

Pressure on the bottom step at the entrance will keep the door open— important to know if you travel with elderly or young passengers.

Many tram stops are situated in the middle of the road, with traffic passing on both sides. Make sure that you take your bearings when you get off. Keep young children close to you.

If a tram has a conductor you must enter by the back door, otherwise you can enter by any of the three doors. Press one of the bells found at regular intervals along the carriage to indicate that you want to get off at the next stop.

Strippenkaart. The strippenkaart is the most general type of ticket sold in the city. It is a strip of small boxes (8, 15, or 45 boxes), one clear box for each transport zone for each journey, so if you intend to travel through two zones the strippenkaart should be stamped in the third box. (The city center zone called the central zone reaches well into the suburbs and covers all of the major attractions in the city.) The strippenkaart can be used by more than one person. Just make sure you get a stamp for each person traveling with you. Each stamp allows one full hour's journeying so you may transfer to another tram or bus within the hour without getting another stamp (the stamp put on your ticket indicates the time it was stamped). If there is a conductor on the bus or tram they will stamp the strippenkaart for you. Strippenkaart are sold on trams and buses, by tobacconists and newsagents, and by VVV offices.

Transport passes. This is one of the most sensible ways of traveling by public transport. Your transport pass will allow you to travel on any form of public transport at any time of day for the duration of the pass. No need to worry about running out of boxes on your strippenkaart. Day passes cost €5.90 per person, but for more days the pass becomes even better value. A 3-day pass costs €10.70, and each additional day costs €2 more. Children's day passes cost €3.60. Also, don't forget about the 1-, 2- or 3-day Amsterdam Pass (see page 59), which allows substantial discounts on museum and transport tickets. Tickets are available from VVV offices and at the GVB ticket office opposite the Central Station.

Amsterdam

Museumboot. Museumboot runs along the canal system between the major sights of the city. It runs at 45-minute intervals (so not as frequently as trams, but is a fun way to travel—and very relaxing). Day tickets cost €13.50 from the Lovers ticket office opposite the entrance to Central Station.

Water taxis. Lovers operate a number of water taxis so that you can personally tailor your trip. It is not for budget travelers—costing from €170 for 30 minutes—but the boats can hold up to 8 people. Wine and cheese parties can be catered for romantic evenings, or you may just wish to book a journey back to your canalside hotel after an evening out. Contact Lovers at Stationplein 8; Tel. 530 1092; fax 530 1099; web site <www.lovers.nl>.

The Metro. Amsterdam metro has three lines which run in linear fashion. They are designed to link the city center with the suburbs and as such are not as useful as other forms of public transport to the visitor touring attractions.

R

RELIGION

The Netherlands is a Christian country with various denominations of Protestant worshippers and Catholic communities. However, strict adherence to church worship has been declining rapidly in recent years and many churches, including several major churches in Amsterdam itself, have been de-consecrated. There is still a small population of Jews who hold synagogue services. As the population of the city has become more multinational there are places of worship for several other religions.

T

TELEPHONE

The international code for The Netherlands is 31 and the city code for Amsterdam is 020. If dialing from outside the country dial 00 31 20 then the seven-digit number.

Most hotels will have international direct dial (IDD) telephones but will charge a high premium for long distance and international calls. Calls using a credit or charge card should not attract any premium.

There are numerous public telephones around the city—most obviously outside the Central and in the major squares—which will take all major credit and charge cards.

Phone cards, available for either €5 or €10, can be purchased from newsagents and tobacconists for local, long distance, and international calls.

To call a number in Amsterdam use the seven-digit number. To call an Amsterdam number from other parts of The Netherlands, dial 020 before the seven-digit number.

To make an international call always dial 00 and then the following country codes:

UK 44	Canada 1
Ireland 353	Australia 61
New Zealand 64	US 1
South Africa 27	

TICKETS

You can obtain tickets for all performances (theater, opera, ballet, etc.) from the VVV Tourist Offices or the Amsterdam Uit Bureau (AUB)-Uitlijn. Contact them at Leidseplein or 621 1211. If you have a credit card they can book tickets for you and send them to your home address or have them waiting for you when you arrive in Amsterdam.

Amsterdam

TIME ZONES

The Netherlands is one hour ahead of Greenwich Mean Time (GMT). If it is noon in Amsterdam here is the time in other cities of the world:

New York 6am.

Sydney 10pm.

London 11am.

Auckland midnight.

Jo'burg 1pm.

TIPPING

Service charges are included in all bar, restaurant and hotel bills, however an extra tip to show gratitude for good service is always accepted. It is appropriate to leave the small change on the table in bars and cafés.

The following situations are still discretionary.

Taxi fares: round up the fare.

Hotel porter: €0.50–1.00 per bag.

Maid: €10 per week.

Lavatory attendant: €0.30—although you may need to pay this as an entry fee.

Tour guide: 10–15%

Concierge: discretionary according to services provided.

TOILETS

There are few public toilet facilities in the city. The department stores and Magna Plaza have them. There is usually a 50c service charge for their use.

Bars and cafés are designated public places but it would be polite to have a coffee or a beer if you use their facilities.

TOURIST INFORMATION

For information before you depart, contact The Netherlands Board of Tourism at the following addresses:

Head Office: Netherlands Bureau voor Toerisme. P.O. Box 458, 2260 MG Leidshendam. The Netherlands; Tel. +31 70 370 5705; fax +31 70 320 1654; web site <www.visitholland.com>.

Canada: 25 Adelaide Street East, suite 710, Toronto ON M5C 1Y2; Tel. 1 888 2-Holland (4665526) in English, Tel. 1 888 Moulins (6685467) in French; fax (416) 363 1470; web site <www.goholland.com>.

South Africa: Export House. P.O. Box 781738; Sandton 2146; Tel. (11) 884 8141; fax (11) 883 5573; e-mail <lvellema@cis.co.za>.

UK and Ireland: Imperial House, 15–19 Kingsway, London WC2B 6UN; Tel. (020) 7539 7950; fax (020) 7539 7953.

US: 355 Lexington Avenue, 21st Floor, NY 10017 New York; Tel. (212) 370 7360; fax (212) 370 9507; web site <www.goholland.com>.

225 North Michigan Avenue, Suite 1854, Chicago, IL 60601; Tel. (312) 819 1636; fax (312) 819 1740; web site <www.goholland.com>.

9841 Airport Boulevard, suite 710, Los Angeles, CA 90045; Tel. (310) 348 9339; fax (310) 348 9344; web site <www.goholland.com>.

For information, maps, hotel bookings, and tickets while in Amsterdam visit the VVV (Amsterdam Tourist Office) at the following addresses. The VVV charges a small fee for many information leaflets and maps.

Stationplein 10: Opposite the entrance to the Central Station.

In the Central Station: Spoor 2.

Leidseplein: at the intersection of Leidsestraat.

The "Stop in Holland" information bureau: located in Schiphol International Airport.

For information by telephone this number is charged at a rate of fl per minute: 900 400 4040.

WEB SITES

Many organizations such as museums and galleries have web sites and these have been included with telephone and fax numbers in the appropriate sections; however, here are some web sites which will give you general information about The Netherlands and Amsterdam which may help you to plan your trip.

<www.noord-holland-tourist.nl> The North Holland tourist office web site has information about Amsterdam and the surrounding areas.

<www.visitholland.com> The Netherlands tourist office, with information about travel to the country and standard tourist information.

WEIGHTS and MEASURES
The Netherlands operates under the metric system.

Length

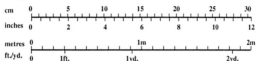

Weight

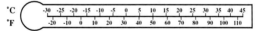

Temperature

YOUTH HOSTELS
There are a number of official and unofficial youth hostels in the city. For more information contact the Dutch Youth Hostel Association (NJHC), Professor Tulpstraat 2, 1018 HA Amsterdam; Tel. 639 2929; fax 639 1099; web site <www.njhc.org>.

Official NJHC hostels offer discounts to members of the International Youth Hostel Association. The main one is at Vondelpark and has 475 beds (Zanspad 5; Tel. 589 8993; fax 598 8955; web site <www.njhc.org/vondelpark>). Reservations recommended at peak times.

Recommended Hotels

A large range of Amsterdam's hotels is graded on a star system by the Benelux Classification System, which rates hotels from five stars down to one star. The Netherlands Board of Tourism has over 200 recommended hotels in the city with star ratings, but there are also many unclassified boarding houses which also represent good value.

Prices are high by international standards but quality is also high. In four- and five-star hotels all rooms will have en-suite facilities; in a three-star hotel only 50% of rooms have their own facilities. Always specify your need for en-suite facilities, if you want them.

The following list recommends hotels in a variety of locations around the city and in all classes. The list concentrates on hotels with a particular character, location, or facility which makes them stand out from the rest.

If you wish to make a phone or fax enquiry/booking dial 00 31 20 before the seven-digit numbers given here.

The following price categories are for one night for two people in a double room with private facilities. Most large hotels charge 5% city tax in addition to room price; smaller hotels include the 5% tax in the price. Most hotels include breakfast in the price of the rooms, however some four and five star hotels charge breakfast separately.

€€€€€	€250+
€€€€	€180–250
€€€	€110–180
€€€	€60–110
€	Under €60

Golden Tulip Barbizon Palace Hotel €€€€€ *Prins Henrikkade 59-72, 1012 AD Amsterdam; Tel. 556 4564; fax 624 3353; web site <www.hotelbook.com/goldentulip>*. This large five-star hotel is situated next to Sint Nicolaaskerk, opposite the Central Station and combines old canal houses with a modern entrance and reception area. All rooms have TV with CNN and Japanese channels, mini-bar, safe, trouser press, and modem jack. 24-hour room service available. Several restaurants including the excellent Vermeer, and fitness room. 274 rooms. Major credit cards.

Hotel de L'Europe €€€€€ *Nieuwe Doelenstraat 2-8, 1012 CP Amsterdam; Tel. 531 1777; fax 531 1778; web site <www.leurope.nl>*. A member of the Leading Hotels of the World group, this centrally located hotel is housed in a building dating from 1896 but beautifully renovated to offer five-star luxury accommodation. The hotel has swimming pool, sauna/solarium, and fitness center. Breakfast is not included in the room price. It also has 50 parking spaces. 100 rooms. Major credit cards.

Hotel Okura Amsterdam €€€€€ *Ferdinand Bolstraat 333, 1072 LH Amsterdam; Tel. 678 7111; fax 671 2344; web site <www.okura.nl>*. Situated out of the city but only a few minutes walk from Museumplein, the Akura has fully equipped health and leisure club. Room facilities include personal voice mail and fax. 370 rooms. Major credit cards.

The Amstel Inter-Continental Amsterdam €€€€€ *Professor Tulpplein 1, 1018 GX, Amsterdam; Tel. 622 6060; fax 622 5808; web site <www.interconti.com>*. The "grande dame" of Amsterdam hotels has benefited from a recent renovation and its rooms are exquisite. Situated directly on the Amstel River the rooms boast CD player, 30-channel TV, and personal voice mail. The hotel has a health and fitness club with pool sauna, gym and massage. 55 rooms. Major credit cards.

The Grand Hotel Krasnapolsky €€€€€ *Dam 9, 1012 JS Amsterdam; Tel. 554 9111; fax 622 8607; web site <www.krasnapolsky.nl>.* This large imposing hotel sits opposite the Royal Palace on Dam Square, in the very heart of the old town. Rooms have safe, hairdryer, mini-bar and TV; the hotel has several restaurants. There is also a pretty interior garden with terrace. The hotel has underground parking facilities. 469 rooms. Major credit cards.

The Grand Westin Demeure €€€€€ *Oudezijds Voorburgwal 197, 1012 EX Amsterdam; Tel. 555 3111; fax 555 3222.* Built in 1578 as a Royal Inn, this building became Amsterdam City Hall following the loss of the Palace in Dam Square and is situated in the very heart of the old city. The exterior is a historic monument while the interior has been refurbished to an extremely high standard. There are excellent spa facilities at extra cost for guests. 182 rooms. Major credit cards.

American Hotel €€€€ *Leidsekade 97, 1017 PN Amsterdam; Tel. 556 3000; fax 556 3001; web site <www.interconti.com>.* Situated in the heart of the bars, restaurants, and clubs of Leidseplein, the American is the favored hotel of celebrities and pop-stars and is also a historic monument. The "Art Deco" rooms are double-glazed to cut out the noise of the bars and cafés below. There is a small gym and sauna. 188 rooms. Major credit cards.

Hotel Pulitzer €€€€ *Prinsengracht 315-331, 1016 HX Amsterdam; Tel. 523 5253; fax 627 6753.* Situated on one of the major canals and comprising 24 historic buildings, the Pulitzer combines history with 5-star comfort. 224 rooms. Major credit cards.

Amsterdam

Le Meridien Apollo €€€€ *Apollolaan 2, 1077 BA Amsterdam; Tel. 673 5922; fax 570 5744; web site <www.meridien.nl>.* Situated 5 minutes walk from Museumplein, towards the RAI conference center, this 5-star hotel is a good base for those who want to be a little way from the hubbub of the city. Situated in a wide canal basin the hotel has wide waterside terraces and marina. Rooms have mini-bar, trouser press, and TV with in-house video. 219 rooms. Major credit cards.

The Park Hotel €€€€ *Stadouderskade 25, 1071 ZD Amsterdam; Tel. 671 7476; fax 664 9455; web site <www.parkhotel.nl>.* Situated across the street from Leidseplein and only minutes from Museumplein, the Park hotel has a bar and restaurant with Dutch cuisine. 187 rooms. Major credit cards.

AMS Lairesse €€€ *De Lairessestraat 7, 1071 NR; Tel. 671 9596; fax 671 1756.* A small budget hotel situated opposite the Concertgebouw, a couple of minutes from Museumplein. The rooms are modern and clean. 34 rooms. Major credit cards.

AMS Museum Hotel €€€ *P.C. Hooftstraat 2, 1071 BX Amsterdam; Tel. 662 1401; fax 673 3918.* Situated near Museumplein and Leidseplein. This is a value option for independent travelers and is also popular with tour groups. The airport shuttle stops in front of the hotel. 110 rooms. Major credit cards.

Canal House €€€ *Keizersgracht 148, 1015 CX Amsterdam; Tel. 622 5185; fax 624 1317; web site <www.canalhouse.nl>.* An intimate family-run hotel in a 17th-century canal house. Each room is individually furnished and breakfast is taken in the old drawing room. Very friendly staff and a small bar. Breakfast included. 26 rooms. Major credit cards.

Die Port van Cleve €€€ *Nieuwezijds Voorburgwal 176-180, 1012 SJ Amsterdam; Tel. 624 4860; fax 622 0240; e-mail <dieportvancleve@wsx.nl>*. Situated just behind the Royal Palace, the hotel has an ornate façade and historic bar with Delft tile decoration. In addition to rooms it also has suites for up to eight people. 120 rooms. Major credit cards.

The Ambassade Hotel €€€ *Herengracht 335-353, 1016 AZ Amsterdam; Tel. 626 2333; fax 624 5321; web site <www.ambassade-hotel.nl>*. Ten historic canal houses have been amalgamated to create The Ambassade situated within a few minutes walk of the town center. The rooms are nicely furnished and the hotel offers 24 hour room service, although it has no restaurant. All rooms have trouser press, mini-bar, safe, and there is a lift to the upper floors. 52 rooms. Major credit cards.

Toro Hotel €€€ *Koningslaan 64, 1075 AG Amsterdam; Tel. 673 7223; fax 675 0031*. Two Edwardian houses set in ample gardens now converted into a stylish hotel. Situated on the south side of Vondelpark. All rooms have TV, safe, and mini-bar. The hotel also has a car park. 22 rooms. Major credit cards.

Tulip Inn Dam Square €€€ *Gravenstraat 12-16, 1012 Amsterdam; Tel. 623 3716; fax 638 1156*. Housed in the building of an old distillery, this cozy hotel has a thoroughly modern interior. It is only minutes from all the activities of central Amsterdam. All rooms have TV and coffee-making facilities. 33 rooms. Major credit cards.

Amstel Botel €€ *Oosterdokskade 2-4, 1011 AE Amsterdam; Tel. 626 4247; fax 639 1952*. The only floating hotel in the city, this modern ship offers compact but tidy and modern rooms, all with TV and interesting views of the city across the water. 176 cabins. Major credit cards.

Hotel Acro €€ *Jan Luykenstraat 44, 1071 CR Amsterdam; Tel. 662 5538; fax 675 0811.* Situated in the vicinity of Museumplein and a few minutes walk from Vondelpark and Leidseplein, The Acro is a modern and functional hotel. 55 rooms. Major credit cards.

Hotel De Filosoof €€ *Anna van den Vondelstraat 6, 1045 GZ Amsterdam; Tel. 683 3013; fax 685 3750.* Situated on the north side of Vondelpark, a little way out of town, this unique hotel is run by a philosopher and she attracts many like-minded guests. Rooms are named after famous philosophers and are individually designed. 25 rooms. Major credit cards.

Hotel Nicolaas Witsen €€ *Nicolaas Witsenstraat 4, 1017 ZH Amsterdam; Tel. 626 6546; fax 620 5113.* Situated on a side street around 15 minutes' walk from the city center and five minutes south of Museumplein. All rooms have TV. This is a good hotel for its class with a very good breakfast. 29 rooms. Major credit cards.

Rho Hotel €€ *Nes 11–23, 1012 KC Amsterdam; Tel. 620 7371; fax 620 7826.* A good value hotel on a quiet street one block back from Rokin. The building was once a theater and retains several original features. Rooms are modern in style. 70 rooms. Major credit cards.

The Seven Bridges €€ *Reguliersgracht 31, 1017 LK Amsterdam; Tel. 623 1329; no fax.* Sitting on one of the prettiest canals, this B&B is one of the most individual in the city with stylishly furnished rooms, stripped floorboards, and antique furniture. No public rooms—breakfast served in your room, steep steps, no young children. 11 rooms. Major credit cards.

Hotel Belga € *Hartenstraat 8, 1016 CB Amsterdam; Tel. 624 9080; fax 623 6862.* Situated in the heart of the old town, the Belga is a good budget option for those who want to be in the center of Amsterdam. Some rooms without private facilities so do specify when you make your booking. All rooms with cable TV and telephone. 10 rooms. Major credit cards.

AT SCHIPHOL AIRPORT

There are many hotels situated around Schiphol international airport, 15 minutes by train from the city center. Most belong to large international groups rather than being independent, "character" hotels. It may however serve your purpose to stay near the airport.

The Sheraton Amsterdam Airport Hotel and Conference Centre €€€€€ *Schiphol Boulevard 101, 1118 BG Schiphol; Tel. 316 4343; fax 316 4399.* This five-star hotel is directly linked to the airport terminal, offering convenient transfer from room to railway station for access to the city. All rooms are soundproofed and the hotel has indoor pool and fitness center. Rooms feature in-house monies and computer games. 24-hour room service and several restaurants. 408 rooms. Major credit cards.

The Dorint Hotel Schiphol €€€€ *Sloterweg 299, 1171 VB Badhoevedorp; Tel. 658 8111; fax 658 8100; e-mail <sales@dha.dorint.nl>.* This hotel, five minutes from Schiphol airport, has free shuttle to the terminal and daily transport to the Rijksmuseum. It also has good connections with motorways and has ample parking. The hotel features restaurant, sauna/solarium, and has squash and tennis courts affiliated to it. 216 rooms. Major credit cards.

Recommended Restaurants

Amsterdam probably has more choice, in terms of types of cuisine, than any city in Europe. Standards are high and prices are reasonable for a major city—although there are very few really budget options. You'll find many small restaurants by simply strolling along the canalside streets and narrow alleyways of the city center.

Since lunch tends to be a snack for the Dutch, most restaurants don't open until the evening. Many restaurants will give you a closing time but are also thoughtful enough to inform you of the kitchen closing time, usually around 90 minutes earlier.

Amsterdam specializes in small, intimate restaurants. Most would prefer that you to make a reservation but many restaurants are used to accommodating walk-in customers. Few restaurants have dress codes but at the higher class establishments it would be advisable to ask.

This list of recommended restaurants concentrates on interesting independent establishments, although a couple of outstanding hotel restaurants are also included.

The following categories are for a three-course dinner per person without drinks. Wine can add considerably to your costs, although many restaurants offer a bottle or carafe of house wine at reasonable cost.

€€€€€	€45 +
€€€€	€36–45
€€€	€27–36
€€	€18–27
€	Up to €18

!zest €€€ *Prinsenstraat 10; Tel. 428 2455.* This restaurant serves "the world on a plate"—so expect anything from spicy Thai salads and curries, to banana cheesecake with maple syrup. Emphasis is on modern techniques and a balancing of flavors.

Open Tuesday–Friday noon–11pm, Saturday 5:30–11pm, Sunday 10am–11pm. Visa cards accepted.

Akita Japanese Restaurant €€€–€€€€ *Rozengracht 228-230; Tel. 625 3254.* Located in the Jordaan area, this restaurant serves a range of hot entrée dishes along with some sushi and sashimi. Would be a good option for those who have not tried Japanese food before as there is not an over-reliance on sushi. Open daily except Monday 6pm–10pm. Major credit cards.

Beddingtons €€€€ *Roelof Hartstraat 6–8; Tel. 676 5201.* A favorite restaurant in the city for many years. The English owner spices up traditional ingredients to excite the taste buds. The elegant minimalist décor is also an excitement. Reservations advised. Open lunch Tuesday–Friday noon–2pm, dinner Monday–Saturday 6pm–10:30pm. Major credit cards.

Bredero € *Oudezijds Voorburgwal 244; Tel. 622 9461.* Situated on a small street one block west of Dam Square, this pancake house is one of the most authentic in the city. It offers a full range of sweet and savory fillings along with cold and toasted sandwiches. Open daily. No credit cards.

Christophe €€€€–€€€€€ *Leliegracht 46; Tel. 625 0807.* Owned by Frenchman Jean-Christophe Royer, this restaurant offers dishes from his native Toulouse, with wines to complement the food. Arguably the best French cuisine in the city. Open daily except Monday, 6:30pm–10:30pm. Major credit cards.

Ciel Bleu (at the Okura Hotel) €€€€€ *Ferdinand Bolstraat 333; Tel. 678 7111; web site <www.okura.nl>.* Set on the 23rd floor of the Okura tower, the Ciel Bleu offers "haute cuisine" and some of the best service in the city. Reservations recommended. Open daily, Monday–Saturday 6:30pm–11pm, Sunday 11:30am–11pm. Major credit cards.

D'Vijff Vleigen €€€€ *Spiustraat 294-302; Tel. 554 6015.* The rather uninviting name of "The Five Flies" should not put you off. This restaurant is over 350 years old. Dutch cuisine with a good range of jenevers. Open daily 5:30pm–10:30pm. Major credit cards.

De Blauwe Hollander €–€€ *Leidsekruisstraat 28, 1017 RJ Amsterdam; Tel. 623 3014.* Hearty Dutch specialities in ample portions at this pretty restaurant. Open dinner only 6:30pm–10pm. Major credit cards.

De Tropen €€–€€€ *Palmgracht 39; Tel. 421 5528; web site <www.dinner-in-amsterdam/de-tropen>.* Fusion cuisine features in this restaurant, and the rattan furniture and naïve Caribbean art give it a tropical feel. Good list of wines from around the world. Open Wednesday–Sunday 6pm–midnight. Major credit cards.

Dynasty €€€ *Reguliersdwarsstraat 30; Tel. 626 8400.* Dynasty has a range of Southeast Asian cuisine, so you have a choice of Thai, Vietnamese, and Chinese dishes. You can choose from the set menus or go à la carte to mix and match your meal from different countries. The food is beautifully prepared from fresh ingredients. The colorful dining room has a ceiling covered in parasols. Open daily except Tuesday, 6pm–11pm. Major credit cards.

Hemelse Modder € *Oude Waal 9, Tel. 624 3203.* This restaurant serves a mixture of vegetarian and meat dishes with French and Italian influences, relying on fresh ingredients. There are

therefore a number of daily specials. Open Tuesday–Sunday
6pm–12.30am. Major credit cards.

het Tuynhuys €€€ *Reguliersdwarsstraat 28; Tel. 627 6603.*
Mediterranean cuisine and bistro-style décor, set in a historic
former coach-house. Beautiful courtyard where you can eat out
in summer. Open daily, lunch (Monday–Friday only)
noon–4.00pm (kitchen open until 2:30pm), dinner 6pm–1am
(kitchen open until 10:30pm). Major credit cards.

In de Waag €–€€ *Nieuwemarkt 4; Tel. 422 7772.* The setting
of this bar/restaurant would be enough to recommend it, set in
the gothic splendor of the old weigh house with its huge beams.
The décor echoes this structure with huge tables for feasting. A
mixed menu of fusion-style dishes. Open daily 10am–1am.
Major credit cards.

Kantijil & de tijger €€ *Spuistraat 291–293; Tel. 620 3074;
web site <www.kantjil.lieverdje.nl>.* Some of the most authentic Indonesian food served in a modern but soothing ambience.
There are also vegetarian dishes on the menu. Open daily
4:30pm–11pm. Major credit cards.

La Rive €€€€–€€€€€ *Professor Tulpplein 1; Tel. 622 6060.*
This formal French restaurant offers a gastronomic extravaganza
and its food is exceptional, it being the only establishment in the
city to have earned two Michelin stars. Excellent wine list. Pretty
riverside setting. Reservations recommended. Open
Monday–Saturday lunch noon–2pm, dinner 6:30pm–10:30pm.
Major credit cards.

Le Garage €€€ *Ruysdaelstraat 54-56; Tel. 679 7176; web site
<www.dinner-in-amsterdam.nl/legarage>.* This exciting

bar/brasserie is owned and operated by Joop Braakhelike who appears in his own cooking program on Dutch TV. The atmosphere is bright and breezy and the food is influenced by the cuisine of France. Open lunch Monday–Friday noon–2pm, dinner daily 6pm–11pm. Major credit cards.

Lucius €€ *Spiustraat 247; Tel. 624 1831.* Lucius specializes in seafood and fish dishes, ranging from huge plates of mussels to salmon to oysters. There is also a range of more exotic or foreign fish such as swordfish. Meat eaters are catered for with a small range of dishes. Open Monday–Saturday 5pm–midnight. Major credit cards.

Manzano €€€ *Rozengracht 106; Tel. 624 5752.* Spanish restaurant with great atmosphere. Everything from a range of tapas with dry sherry to authentic paella. Relaxed bistro-style atmosphere. Open Wednesday–Sunday 5:30pm–midnight. Major credit cards.

Plaka €€ *Egelantierstraat 124; Tel. 627 9338.* Authentic Greek cuisine in lively taverna atmosphere. Plaka specialize in oven-cooked dishes such as *moussaka* or *stifado*, to *mezedhes* accompanied by *ouzo*. Open daily 4pm–10:30pm. Major credit cards.

Pygma-lion €€ *Nieuwe Spiegelstraat 5a; Tel. 420 7022.* This funky South African bistro serves exotic meats such as ostrich, although there are also more mainstream choices, along with salads and sandwiches. Open daily, Monday 11am–3pm, Tuesday–Sunday 11am–10pm. Major credit cards.

Restaurant Vermeer (at the Golden Tulip Barbizon Palace Hotel) €€€€ *Prins Henrikkade 59-72; Tel. 556 4885.* One of the finest restaurants in Amsterdam which has a French menu with world influences. Open lunch Monday–Friday noon–3pm, dinner Monday–Saturday 6pm–10:30pm. Major credit cards.

Rosa's Cantina €€–€€€ *Reguliersdwarsstraat 38–40; Tel. 625 9797.* Busy Mexican restaurant serving large portions of Tex-Mex cuisine. Enchiladas, tortillas, fajitas, and sizzling chimichangas, with a range of burgers, along with pitchers of margaritas. Open daily 5:30pm–11.30pm. Major credit cards.

Sluizer €€€ *Utrechtstraat 43-45; Tel. 626 3557.* The plain wooden tables and simple elegant decoration in Sluizer could grace any French bistro. You'll find two restaurants in one here with a choice of excellent seafood—mussels a speciality—or French cuisine. Open lunch Monday–Friday noon–2pm, dinner daily 6pm–10:30pm. Major credit cards.

Tara Irish Pub € *Rokin 89; Tel. 625 1498.* Authentic pub atmosphere with pub food such as beef and ale pies, and hot-pots. Good, hearty, and filling. Open daily 11am–11pm, later on weekends. Major credit cards.

Tom Yam €€ *Staalstraat 22; Tel. 622 5933.* Wonderfully authentic Thai food prepared by a well-known Dutch restaurateur who turned his hand from Continental to Asian cuisine. The restaurant is small but the wait will be worth it. Open daily 6pm–10pm. Major credit cards.

Treasure $–€€ *Nieuwezijds Voorburgwal 115; Tel. 626 0915.* Probably the most authentic Chinese cuisine in the city, with several regional styles on the menu, this restaurant sits in the heart of the Chinese Quarter. There is also a dim-sum bar. Open daily except Wednesday noon–10:30pm. Major credit cards.

INDEX